# EARLY CHILDHOOD EDUCATION SERIES

Sharon Ryan, *Editor*

ADVISORY BOARD: *Celia Genishi, Doris Fromberg, Carrie Lobman, Rachel Theilheimer, Dominic Gullo, Amita Gupta, Beatrice Fennimore, Sue Grieshaber, Jackie Marsh, Mindy Blaise, Gail Yuen, Alice Honig, Betty Jones, Stephanie Feeney, Stacie Goffin, Beth Graue*

*(continued)*

# Multicultural Teaching in the Early Childhood Classroom

## Approaches, Strategies, and Tools, Preschool–2nd Grade

*Mariana Souto-Manning*

Teachers College
Columbia University
New York and London

*Association for*
**Childhood Education
International**™
Washington, D.C.

Published simultaneously by Teachers College Press, 1234 Amsterdam Avenue, New York, NY 10027, and the Association for Childhood Education International, 1101 16th Street, N.W., Suite 300, Washington, D.C., 20036, www.acei.org

Figure 7.1, "100% Kids," by Vivian Vasquez's http://www.bazmakaz .com/100kids/2007

*Library of Congress Cataloging-in-Publication Data*

Souto-Manning, Mariana.
    Multicultural teaching in the early childhood classroom : approaches, strategies, and tools, preschool–2nd grade / Mariana Souto-Manning.
        pages cm. — (Early childhood education series)
    Includes bibliographical references and index.
    ISBN 978-0-8077-5405-4 (pbk. : alk. paper) — ISBN 978-0-8077-5406-1 (hardcover : alk. paper)
    1. Multicultural education—Study and teaching—United States. 2. Early childhood education—United States. I. Title.
    LC1099.3.S635 2013
    370.117–dc23

2012042620

ISBN 978-0-8077-5405-4 (paperback)
ISBN 978-0-8077-5406-1 (hardcover)

Printed on acid-free paper
Manufactured in the United States of America

20  19  18  17  16  15  14        8  7  6  5  4  3  2

*I dedicate this book to my children*
*Lucas and Thomas*

*Thank you for your love, support, and belief*
*that everything is possible. I am committed*
*to making this world a better place and am*
*thrilled that you join and inspire me every day.*

# Contents

# Acknowledgments

As someone who learned the word *peacock* as an adult from an Eric Carle book a little over 15 years ago, I am thankful for teachers who refused to give up and who saw diversities as strengths. I am only where I am because of them. The word *peacock* used to fit uneasily into my mouth. I didn't know much English—and never thought I would be able to write an essay in English, much less books. Because of such caring teachers, I became an early childhood teacher in the United States. The teachers who inspired me have much in common with the teachers who are featured in this book.

This book features the teaching of brilliant and caring teachers who refuse to give up on the children they teach—even in difficult times. These teachers are committed to equity and multicultural education even in light of the standardization of curriculum and teaching brought about by No Child Left Behind and Race to the Top. They are (alphabetized by first name as is common in my native Brazil): Carol Branigan Felderman, Dahlia Bouari, Dana Frantz Bentley, Henry Padrón Morales, Janice Baines, Maria Helena Mendonça Buril, and Mary Cowhey.

Through teaching, all of these teachers enact their belief in multicultural education in a variety of ways, yet they are each committed to enacting equitable education, learning from and with the children they teach. I met each of these amazing human beings and caring teachers over the course of the last 15 years and knowing them has enriched my life in significant ways. If it weren't for their teaching, this book would not exist. The stories in this book are their stories. I am forever indebted to each of them. I am inspired by their talk and by their walk. May every child have such a committed and caring teacher! I am thankful to all teachers who—like the teachers featured in this book—remain committed to fostering a more equitable society through their actions every day. I also offer my deep gratitude to the children and families portrayed in the pages of this book.

I thank Sharon Ryan, Early Childhood Education Series Editor, for inviting me to consider writing this book and Marie Ellen Larcada, Acquisitions Editor, for her encouragement, care, and follow through. I offer my warmest gratitude to Celia Genishi for reading the very first draft of the proposal I submitted to Teachers College Press—her critical feedback and constant support were (and continue to be) essential. I acknowledge Susan Liddicoat for her masterful edits, for her patience, and care. I thank Aureliano Vazquez for his support in the production of this book.

I am grateful to Teachers College for the gift of time. President Susan Fuhrman and Provost Thomas James supported me through a generous research leave—during which I wrote this book. In addition, I thank my dear colleagues A. Lin Goodwin and Celia Oyler who were quick to say no for me when I hesitated—and firmly reminded others and me that a research leave is for research. I thank Britt Hamre for the words of encouragement and for the "go for it" attitude, whether over a cup of coffee, email, or Facebook. In addition, I am truly fortunate to have very supportive colleagues and friends at Teachers College, Columbia University, the University of Georgia, and the University of South Carolina–Columbia—many of whom cannot be named here. I thank each and every one of them.

I thank all students with whom I have taught and learned over the years—and across geographic boundaries. At Teachers College, I offer my heartfelt thanks to Ranita Cheruvu, Eileen Blanco, Tara Lencl, Haemin Yu, Marisa Calubaquib-Chin, Carmina Makar, Sarah Zalcmann, and Ysaaca Axelrod for their enthusiasm and support as I developed the idea of writing this specific book. A number of my current and former (early childhood and university) students have made important contributions to this book—here I acknowledge each and every one of them.

I affectionately acknowledge my academic family, Marcelle Haddix, Valerie Kinloch, Detra Price-Dennis, Mary Rojas, Yolanda Sealey-Ruiz, and Benji Chang. I thank each and every one of them for keeping it real, giving me support when I needed it, for listening to me and caring for me, but also challenging me to continue growing as a person and professional and for asking hard questions. They inspire me! A huge thanks to the National Council of Teachers of English Cultivating New Voices Program family—specifically to those who I had the honor to formally mentor, Margarita Zisselsberger and Ebony Elizabeth Thomas—and be mentored by—Celia Genishi. I also thank master teacher-researchers who have supported not only me over the years, but also the teachers who are featured in this book: Susi Long, Sonia Nieto, and Vivian Vasquez.

Because I know how important one's history is, I especially acknowledge my family—where I came from. My mother Suely; my brothers, Thiago and Bernardo; *Titia;* and my sister-in-law Juliana, who have supported me over the years and continue to do so from afar. To *Papai*, I owe my vision of social activism to him. I still remember the day he introduced me to Freirean culture circles—when I was barely a teenager. In addition, he instilled a sense of social justice in me by taking me to political events regarding Brazil's redemocratization (*Diretas Já* and the many meetings that preceded it) when I was still in diapers. His influence endures. I wish he were alive to see this book—and the work I do. In addition to my family in Brazil, I acknowledge the love and support of my NYC family, in particular, *Lita*.

I offer my greatest gratitude and love to my spouse, Dwight. Without ever voicing a complaint, he supported my work across time, read multiple sections of this book, and patiently offered his candid feedback. I thank our sons Lucas and Thomas for their energy, enthusiasm, and excitement—and for their love every day. I dedicate this book to them!

Finally, I offer my gratitude to those who read this book. I hope that you find the stories in this book inspiring and hopeful. I hope that you start reinventing the strategies and tools presented here in your own setting. I hope to hear from you!

# CHAPTER 1

# Multicultural Approaches, Strategies, and Tools for Teaching Young Children

Is it necessary to engage in multicultural education in the early years? Why? How young is too young to consider multiple cultures? Is multicultural education something nice to do or a necessary practice that must be embraced in early childhood settings?

There may be many reasons for dismissing the need for multicultural education in the early years—because it may be deemed to be too political or beyond children's understandings and experiences, for example. Yet, as you think about these questions, I invite you to consider the following real-life scenarios:

> 3-year-old Antonia went to a toy store with her preschool class to buy a doll. Despite the fact that her own skin is brown and her hair is black, she spearheaded the argument for buying a White doll with blond hair because "she is prettier."

> Two 4-year-old children—Felicia and Tom—engaged in pretend play in their preschool classroom. They found two stuffed bunnies—one pink and one blue—and designated the pink one to be a girl and the blue one to be a boy. Then, when they needed a villain, Tom ran across the classroom and found a Black doll to play the "monster."

> Two 5-year-old girls are playing in their PreK classroom. There is one princess dress and both girls want to wear it and pretend to be princesses. Catherine (a White girl with blond hair and blue eyes) tells Darcy (a Chinese American girl): "You know, real princesses have blond hair. And they have blue eyes. So, you are not a real princess. Give me the dress!"

By considering these scenarios we are reminded that from a very young age, children may begin displaying gender and racial preferences (or associations) and may develop prejudices. They remind us of the need for multicultural education in the early years (Banks, 1993; Derman-Sparks & Ramsey, 2011; Genishi & Goodwin, 2008; Ramsey, 2004). As teachers committed to a just society, it is our responsibility to engage in multicultural teaching in the early childhood classroom. By ignoring or tolerating events such as the ones in the examples above, we teachers are reinforcing stereotypes.

1

As you think about the question, How young is too young? I ask you to consider many children's preferences for gentle European lullabies and classical music as opposed to the stronger beat of African and Latin American rhythms. Is this nature or nurture? Do we socialize children from a very young age into privileging Whiteness? How about their identification of colors—pink for girls and blue for boys? How young do they start identifying? A study conducted by Birgitte Vittrup at the Children's Research Lab at the University of Texas documented that children younger than age 1 can show racial preferences, associating Whiteness with niceness and darker skin colors with unpleasant feelings. Findings showed that children as young as 6 months judge others based on skin color (Bronson & Merryman, 2009). So—how young is too young? A child is never too young to engage in educational experiences that foster equity and justice (Banks, 1993). The real questions are:

- How can teachers of young children engage in teaching multiculturally?
- What are some of the approaches, strategies, and tools that can be used to foster multicultural learning communities in the early years?

In this chapter, we focus on these questions. We consider how the dimensions of multicultural education can come into focus and shape curricula and teaching—that is, the ways in which race, ethnicity, income, language, culture, ability, gender, and sexuality frame and are framed in teaching and learning (Nieto, 1999). But before we delve into this journey, I invite you to examine what is meant by multicultural education, especially because there is much talk about the concepts of multicultural education and not many examples of tools, practices, and strategies in action.

## WHAT IS MULTICULTURAL EDUCATION?

Ask a group of teachers "What is multicultural education?" and you may get as many different responses as there are individuals in the group. Because there are multiple ways to define and engage in multicultural education, it is rare that any two early childhood teachers will share exactly the same understanding. Some teachers conceive of multicultural education as adding so-called "multicultural materials" to their classrooms. A specific example would be purchasing "multicultural dolls" (often identified as such in educational catalogues) and adding them to the dramatic play area or purchasing and adding African drums to the music area or box. Some believe that such actions would take care of multicultural education and honor diversities. This is not what I mean by multicultural education in this book, as merely adding new materials does not necessarily comprise a change in teaching and learning, nor in the interactions and beliefs present in a classroom (De Gaetano, Williams, & Volk, 1998; Ramsey & Williams, 2003).

Considering the scenarios that open this chapter, I ask that you imagine the addition of an African American or Latina/Latino doll to Antonia's classroom or to Felicia and Tom's classroom. Do you think this action would foster multicultural education? Specifically, do you believe that Antonia would play with a brown doll if it had inadvertently been added to the play area? Or would Antonia choose the blond doll because "she is prettier"? Would Felicia and Tom see the doll as an equally worthy member of their fantasy play or would they cast the dark-skinned doll as a villain or a monster? I hope that these questions "trouble" the practice of merely adding "multicultural materials" to the classroom as education for equity. In these classrooms, a darker doll may merely serve as an accessory to (or way of illustrating) children's perceptions and stereotypes about people of color.

Getting beyond the addition of multicultural materials to the early childhood classroom, some other teachers of young children may reflect on classroom climate and ways of teaching. They may focus on rethinking and transforming the curriculum and their teaching, making them more equitable and thus engaging in multicultural education. While this may sound wonderful, how do we implement it? "How?" is the question asked by many teachers. To address this question, in this book I focus on both curriculum and teaching as we explore approaches, strategies, and tools for fostering multicultural learning communities in the early years. And because there are multiple understandings and many misunderstandings of multicultural education (such as defining multicultural education as the exploration of foreign cultures), it is important to define what I mean by multicultural education. In doing so, we consider key premises of multicultural education from a critical perspective.

## Defining Multicultural Education

There are many definitions of multicultural education. James Banks and Cherry McGee Banks (2004) defined multicultural education as "a field of study designed to increase educational equity for all students" (p. xii). In refining his definition, James Banks (2004) developed five dimensions of multicultural education:

1. Content integration (bringing together multiple cultural perspectives, knowledges, and experiences in teaching and learning)
2. Knowledge construction process (locating the social, cultural, and historical construction of knowledge—coming to trouble culture-free notions of knowledge, teaching, and learning)

3. Prejudice reduction (developing positive cross-cultural and intergroup attitudes and actions in the classroom while troubling privileges and seeking to move away from deficit perspectives)
4. Equity pedagogy (implementing transformative teaching strategies that honor children as worthy, capable, and unique human beings who are members of diverse communities and families)
5. Empowerment of school culture and social structure (changing the status of diverse groups in schools, fostering more equitable experiences in terms of power and status).

Geneva Gay (1994) defined multicultural education as:

> Policies, programs, and practices employed in schools to celebrate cultural diversity. It builds on the assumption that teaching and learning are invariably cultural processes. . . . As used in this definition, celebration means to know, believe, accept, value, use, and promote cultural diversity as a normal feature of humankind, a characteristic trait of U.S. society, and an essential component of quality education for all students. Effective implementation of multicultural education requires a combination of the personal attitudes and values of educators, curriculum content, instructional methods and materials, classroom climates, and the participation of individuals at all levels of the educational enterprise. (p. 17)

Sonia Nieto (2002) defined multicultural education critically, within a complex sociopolitical context, inviting us to acknowledge and reaffirm the need for multicultural education which

> challenges and rejects racism and other forms of discrimination in schools and society and accepts and affirms the pluralism (ethnic, racial, linguistic, religious, economic, and gender, among others) that students, their communities, and teachers reflect. Multicultural education permeates schools' curriculum and instructional strategies, as well as interactions among teachers, students, and families, and the very way that schools conceptualize the nature of teaching and learning. Because it uses critical pedagogy as its underlying philosophy and focuses on knowledge, reflection, and action (praxis) as the basis for social change, multicultural education promotes democratic principles of social justice . . . is antiracist . . . [and] important for all students. (pp. 29–30)

From a critical perspective, multicultural education focuses on challenging the idea of diverse individuals having deficits (as lacking something or needing to be fixed) or as being inferior. Multicultural education is about fostering and forming equitable and socially just communities (Ramsey & Williams, 2003). Multicultural education "uses the transformation of self and school as . . . metaphor[s] and point[s] of departure for the transformation of society. Ultimately, social justice and equity in schools can, and should, mean social justice and equity in society" (Gorski, 2010b, p. 1).

## Transforming Education

In this book, I approach multicultural education as a progressive stance for reimagining and transforming education. Multicultural teaching is good teaching for all students. This approach to education holistically critiques and responds to discriminatory policies and practices in education. It involves contextualizing, historicizing, and problematizing inequities in classrooms and beyond (Souto-Manning, 2010b). Thus, instead of finding fault with traditionally disenfranchised families, it is important to work toward eradicating teaching practices that disenfranchise—teaching practices that are not inclusive of multiple perspectives and points of view (Derman-Sparks & Ramsey, 2011). As you begin or continue to transform your own classroom practices, ask yourself:

- Do I tend to find fault with students of color or other students and families from traditionally disenfranchised groups (e.g., gay and lesbian families, low-income)?
- Do I critically examine ways in which (pre)school policies and my teaching practices influence disparities in educational outcome?
- Do I tend to blame individual students and their families for educational failure, or do I tend to examine how larger societal factors (health care, wages, housing) influence disparities in educational outcome?

(adapted from Gorski, 2010a)

While these are difficult questions, it is important to be honest because naming and recognizing inequitable issues, practices, and mindsets which influence teaching and learning are necessary to promoting change (Freire, 1970).

## THE CONTEXT OF MULTICULTURAL EDUCATION

While the focus of this book is on multicultural curriculum and teaching, it is important to consider many issues beyond the classroom walls. These issues include discourses such as readiness, early intervention, tracking, standardized testing, or funding discrepancies. For example, many diverse young children are identified as needing intervention, as being academically behind from a very young age, thereby affecting their educational opportunities and futures (Souto-Manning, 2010c). Standardized testing (and tests that seek to identify children with disabilities, for example) often honor White ways of being, talking, and behaving (Derman-Sparks & Ramsey, 2011; Fennimore, 2000; Genishi & Dyson, 2009), thus disadvantaging children of color and speakers of languages other than Mainstream American English, the term I prefer for the so-called "Standard English." Further, there are many funding discrepancies that allow wealthier school districts to provide better educational opportunities and environments for their students, yet those with lower tax bases have to fight for federal funds in order to supplement their budgets. Often such federal funding comes at the cost of adopting very high-pressure and child-unfriendly curricula (Genishi & Dyson, 2009, 2012). In private childcare centers, the tuition typically determines the kind of training teachers receive, the teacher-child ratios, and the materials and physical area available to children (Kagan & Kauerz, 2012). Families who cannot afford to pay such tuition often rely on kin networks, on neighbors, or on whoever is available to keep their kids for the lowest price (Kagan, Kauerz, & Tarrant, 2008). Thus, while well known at the K–12 level (Kozol, 1991), these stark inequalities are also an issue for childcare in the first 5 years of a child's life. Whether in the first 5 years of a child's life or at the K–12 level, such inequitable educational opportunities must be changed (Banks, 1994; McLaren, 1994).

Educational change starts in the classroom through the construction of multicultural learning communities (Nieto, 1999). Yet, it is part of—and hopefully will lead to—a larger societal transformation in which we closely explore, problematize, critique, and seek to change the ways in which society and education maintain the current power structure—for example, over-valuing of Mainstream American English, marginalizing African American Language and Spanish, and offering privileged educational opportunities to children of higher income families (Derman-Sparks & Ramsey, 2011; Gregory, Long, & Volk, 2004; Ramsey, 2004).

We know that there is inequity in education. Proof of inequity is that real estate ads include school attendance zones to lure families who can afford to move to areas where their children will attend better schools. Yet, this segregates children, providing better educational experiences to children whose families have higher incomes and leaving no choice (or very little choice) for families who are not able to move in search of a better school. Attendance zones and funding formulas further reify the segregation of schools. This plight is illustrated by the desperation of families portrayed in the motion picture *Waiting for Superman* (Chilcott & Guggenheim, 2010).

For example, in less than 30 minutes on one New York City subway line, one may travel from one of the poorest congressional districts (the South Bronx) to one of the richest districts in the country (Upper East Side, Manhattan). It may seem easy to move—or even commute to and from school over such a short distance if it weren't for the property prices and school zoning issues. One-bedroom apartments near 59th Street and Fifth Avenue are available for around $3.5 million. Two-bedroom apartments in the South Bronx can cost less than 10% of that price. While the same school system serves both areas, the schools on the Upper East Side are performing far better than schools in the South Bronx. Providing both of these areas with the same public funding does not comprise equity. Equity is not simply allocating the same amount of money per student. Equity is based on fairness and promotes educational opportunities which foster the success of all students (Nieto, 1996).

While this example illustrates a stark inequity situated in New York City, inequities in terms of access to quality education and well-resourced (pre)schools are present throughout the country and the world (Mansell & Curtis, 2009). Let's consider what many refer to as "White flight." Over 30 years ago, *Time* magazine reported White flight as a voluntary form of racially and socioeconomically segregating schools (Education, 1978). Families who were socioeconomically able to do so moved according to school attendance zones, thus deserting many schools serving populations that have traditionally been marginalized and disadvantaged—for example, children of color, immigrant children, English language learners, children with special needs, children of low-income families. While attendance zones are often portrayed as equal, they are not equitable. Families who have money to move can afford to choose the schools their children attend. Families who do not are relegated and often segregated. Thus, while multicultural education addresses injustices and inequities that happen in the classroom, it is also about social justice at large.

## DOING MULTICULTURAL EDUCATION

Multicultural education seeks to support a diversities perspective (Carter & Goodwin, 1994), affirming diversities as an essential aspect of a democratic society (Nieto, 2000). Multicultural education seeks to respect the humanity of every person, prioritizing teachers' and children's personal, practical knowledge as foundational to promoting change in early childhood settings and beyond. Yet, despite its promise, little is truly known about how to *do* multiculturalism in schools (Hoffman, 1996; Sleeter & Bernal, 2003). As I sought to document multicultural teaching in early childhood classrooms, I wanted to make sure that the practices portrayed in this book helped us gain insights into how to *do* multicultural education in early educational settings, yet did not fall into the trivialized infusion of celebrations and commemorations while ignoring the everyday issues and tensions experienced by diverse children and their families. The teachers portrayed in the following chapters, instead of thinking of young children in terms of what they were not able to do in their classrooms (in terms of deficits), engaged them in rich multicultural educational experiences that empowered children to understand themselves in relation to others. In situated and particular ways, each teacher engaged in critical multicultural education, considering the dynamic and interrelated concepts of culture, identity, and experience within a critical analysis of power structures and teaching.

This book is not meant to be a how-to guide, inclusive of every possible way of teaching multiculturally. Such a task would be impossible, as multicultural teaching does not come in ready packages or have a specific formula. This book presents a sample of approaches, strategies, and tools that are powerful and in action, in real classrooms, allowing you to learn about the ways early childhood teachers are getting started and continuing to transform education in hopeful ways in a world that at times seems pretty gloomy (and standardized and test-driven).

While this book proposes a collection of approaches, strategies, and tools in action, it takes a critical and situated perspective. By doing so, it problematizes dominant views of learning and troubles false boundaries and separations—such as home and school literacy practices, or culturally responsive teaching and academic rigor. In addition, it recognizes that strategies and tools will "look and sound different in different social and cultural circumstances" (Dyson & Genishi, 2005, p. 4), in different classrooms.

As you enter these teachers' classrooms, you will see that homes and communities are part of the classrooms, part of teaching and learning. For example, in Janice Baines's 1st-grade classroom, you will see that culturally responsive teaching does not have to come at the expense of academic rigor and meeting the Common Core State Standards. In Mary Cowhey's 2nd-grade classroom, you will see family and community members as teachers. You will see many more examples of how these unique teachers deal with issues of power, culture, identities, and privileges in their own classrooms, taking a critical multicultural stance *with* the children they teach.

Together, the approaches explored in this book provide fertile grounds for critical multicultural education to take root in early childhood settings. This is because the approaches, tools, and strategies employed by the featured teachers consider a variety of perspectives and knowledges, while honoring situated experiences through listening to the voices, knowledge, and interests of children. The tools and strategies they employ locate social, cultural, and historical contexts and discourses shaping everyday situations, and honor multiple viewpoints and backgrounds. Through meaningful learning experiences these amazing teachers engage in collective actions and strive to foster more equitable educational experiences.

## LOOKING AHEAD

This chapter provided an overview of multicultural education, situating this book within the body of work by early childhood educators who prioritize multicultural approaches to teaching young children. In Chapter 2, I invite you to examine and rethink your own assumptions and beliefs about young children's understandings of issues of privilege (Banks, 1993). The six chapters that follow each exemplify ways in which specific multicultural approaches, strategies, and tools have been used in early childhood settings: interviews (Chapter 3), critical inquiry (Chapter 4), culture circles with multicultural literature (Chapter 5), community resources and home literacies (Chapter 6), technology (Chapter 7), and storytelling and story acting (Chapter 8). In each chapter, we enter early childhood classrooms where critical multicultural education is enacted and learn from the experiences of teachers as they reflect on their practices—not only the plusses but the stresses and conflicts they experienced as they engaged in multicultural teaching and learning.

As a multicultural text, this book invites you to consider a variety of approaches from diverse classrooms and listen to the voices of early childhood teachers who employ such strategies and tools in their own classrooms. The teachers featured in the pages of this book are teaching in Massachusetts, New York, Virginia, South Carolina, and Georgia. They teach in Head Start, preschool, kindergarten, 1st, and 2nd grades. They are White, African American, Latina/o, and Asian American. They are mostly women. Some entered the profession 2 years ago, and some have been in the classroom for nearly three decades. They are between their 20s and their 60s. Some of them grew up close to where they teach—some did not. They have varying academic degrees and preparation—from an associate's degree to a doctorate. They have varying degrees of fluency in Mainstream American English, African American Language, Spanish, Portuguese, and Arabic. They are monolingual, bilingual, and trilingual. Their voices convey a variety of accents—and unique perspectives all committed to honoring the brilliance of every child. They teach in public and private settings. They are bound by standards and Title I assessments; they are freed by play-based approaches to learning. Yet, they all negotiate spaces to engage in multicultural teaching. Because their practices and voices are unique, each chapter is unique. The scenarios shared here were constructed from interviews, observations, teacher research, and collaborations which took place over the course of 6 years (2006–2012), although each chapter portrays learning journeys which lasted no more than 1 academic year. In using teachers' actual names, I first introduce them by their first and last names. Thereafter, the name their students used with them is adopted. To protect their identities, fictitious names (pseudonyms) were given to all children, with the exception of Joe Marks, Jeyleene, Evan, and Hannalise in Mary Cowhey's classroom.

The final chapter (Chapter 9) provides a summary of the multicultural tools, strategies, and approaches presented throughout the book and invites you to reflect on the possibilities of teaching multiculturally—even in light of mandated curricula and highly prescriptive programs—by reframing existing resources (what's already present in your classroom or school). I draw on the expertise of a Latina Head Start teacher and offer insights for creating "wiggle room," envisioning spaces of possibilities, and teaching multiculturally in contexts that are not inviting to multicultural practices.

As there are multiple cultures shaping individual human beings, there are many ways to engage in multicultural education in the early years. And not all of them are explored here; see also the resources listed at the ends of Chapters 3–8. As you read about the many strategies and tools that can foster multicultural learning communities presented in this book, I hope that you will rethink, adapt, reimagine, and reinvent some of these strategies, making them authentic and relevant to your own settings and classrooms.

# CHAPTER 2

# Multicultural Education as Transformative Education

Multicultural education is grounded in ideals of social justice, educational equity, and a dedication to providing educational experiences that allow every child to reach his or her full potential as a learner and as a socially aware and active being (Banks, 1996; Nieto, 1999). Multicultural education acknowledges that teachers, classroom communities, and schools as a whole are essential to laying the foundation for the transformation of society and the elimination of injustice. The aim of multicultural education is to affect positive social change, to transform society and schools through education.

## THE PROGRESSION OF INTERRELATED TRANSFORMATION

Multicultural education, when conceived as education for transformation, involves three layers of interrelated transformation: (1) of self, (2) of teaching, and (3) of society (Gorski, 2010b).

### Transformation of Self

To teach multiculturally, one starts by self-identifying as a cultural being. Many teachers may not think of themselves as cultural beings (Derman-Sparks & Ramsey, 2011; Goodwin & Genor, 2008)—especially those who grew up in cultures that are not deemed to be "different" (read White, middle- or upper-class, speakers of Mainstream American English). Culture may signal something exotic or foreign for some. Yet, we are all cultural beings, and it is important to identify the cultural threads that make up the fabric of our own selves. Unless we come to understand how our culture shaped and continues to shape who we are, we will not be able to teach multiculturally—we will continue to honor our own culture as the norm, and teach in (mono)culturally specific ways (Goodwin, Cheruvu, & Genishi, 2008). I invite you to self-identify as a cultural being by considering the following questions:

- Who am I? That is, what are the cultural threads that make up the fabric of who I am today?
- Am I ignoring the existence of differences as a way to avoid addressing the difficult issues related to them?

If we are not able to identify as cultural beings, we are not able to identify the positions of privilege we occupy—such as being White, having grown up in an economically comfortable household, speaking Mainstream American English, being heterosexual, or being Christian. I know that it is easy to avoid asking questions such as:

- What privileges have allowed me to be where I am?
- What privileges have shaped who I am, what I think, and how I teach?

After all, the prevalent myth employed to justify privilege is that we are part of a meritocracy—that if one works hard enough, he or she will succeed. Yet, I invite you to engage in such self-examination. The purpose of this self-examination is to understand how specific cultural experiences and identities can advantage or disadvantage one within society. Further, this self-examination is aimed at understanding how your perceptions and beliefs may be positioning your students' cultural backgrounds as advantages and/or disadvantages (Derman-Sparks & Ramsey, 2011). Indeed, the values we attribute to personal, social, political, cultural, and educational factors affect the success or failure of students in our classrooms (Nieto & Bode, 2011).

In addition to coming to an understanding of our own selves as cultural beings, as educators, we have a dual responsibility to also engage in a critical and continual process of examining how our socializations and biases inform our teaching and thus affect the educational experiences of our students (Freire, 1998). We have the responsibility to examine how we perceive the people and happenings around us. Only when we have a sense of how our own perceptions are developed in relation to our experiences will we begin to understand the world and successfully navigate our relationships with the young children we teach. We have a responsibility to young children to work toward recognizing, acknowledging, and eliminating our prejudices, examining who is (and who is not) being reached by our teaching, and relearning who we are. After all, the ways we make sense of our identities affect our students' learning experiences.

In the spirit of critically examining our socializations and biases, I ask you to take a few minutes and seriously consider the following questions. They will help you examine your commitment to multicultural education.

- Does every child who enters my classroom have an opportunity to achieve success to her or his fullest capability regardless of race, ethnicity, sex, gender identity, sexual orientation, religion, socioeconomic status, home language, dis/ability, and other social and cultural identifiers? Do I tend to advantage children whose race, ethnicity, or religion are aligned with my own?
- Do I understand that equity requires eliminating disparities of access to opportunities and resources—what some might call fairness or justice? And, sometimes—when I offer equality (giving everyone the same thing)—do I fail to meet this requirement?
- When I advocate for equity in educational access do I take into account all types of "access"? Do I consider physical access as well as social, economic, and cultural access?

Critical multicultural educators engage in a constant process of self-examination and transformation—asking if we are advantaging some children over others and how our own upbringing and experiences are influencing our teaching and the learning climate in our classrooms.

## Transformation of Teaching

Multicultural education calls for a critical examination of all aspects of schooling (Grant & Sleeter, 1990). Here, we focus on two aspects of transforming teaching—fostering student-centered ways of teaching and designing a multicultural curriculum.

*Fostering student-centered ways of teaching.* One of the key premises of multicultural education is that the experiences of students (and their families and communities) are brought to the forefront in the classroom, making learning active, interactive, relevant, and engaging (Nieto, 2010; Souto-Manning, 2010b). Thus, traditional teaching approaches—teachers being the sole experts in the classroom, transmission of knowledge from teacher to student—are deconstructed to examine how they contribute to and support educational injustice and inequity (Freire, 1970; Nieto, 1999). Known inequitable practices like tracking—determining who is ready for kindergarten (even if informally), early intervention indicators, standardized test scores, and school rankings—are questioned, critically examined, and contested.

To engage in student-centered ways of teaching, all aspects of teaching and learning in schools are re-examined and redirected to the students themselves. We will see many examples of student-centered ways of teaching in the forthcoming chapters, where emphasis is placed on critical thinking, learning skills, and deep social awareness as well as the contextualization and problematization of facts and figures—acknowledging that knowledge is culturally shaped (Grant & Sleeter, 1990). Multicultural teaching provides all students with the opportunity to reach their full potential as learners.

*Designing a multicultural curriculum.* All curricula need to be analyzed for accuracy and completeness. "A multicultural curriculum rests on two ideals: (a) equal opportunity and (b) cultural pluralism" (Grant, 2008, p. 895). Analysis of curricula may begin by asking questions such as:

- Who told this story?
- Is there another possible narrative?
- What are other perspectives?
- Are there additional points of view or explanations?

To fashion a multicultural curriculum, all subjects are presented from multiple perspectives as related to accuracy and completeness (De Gaetano, Williams, & Volk, 1998; Ladson-Billings, 1994). Here, an "inclusive curriculum" means including the voices of the students in the classroom, their families, and communities. Thus, educational materials should be inclusive of diverse voices and perspectives (Bishop, 2007; Derman-Sparks & Ramsey, 2011). As part of a multicultural curriculum, students are encouraged to think critically about materials and media and consider questions such as:

- Whose voices are they hearing or not hearing?
- Why did that company produce that film?
- Who wrote this book?
- What biases is the author bringing to her or his writing?

The idea of published media as sanctioning "real" and "worthy" knowledge is thus deconstructed.

In addition to inviting you to ask questions, this book invites you to consider multiple ways early childhood teachers have engaged in constructing a multicultural curriculum and will shed light onto the ways in which you can bring a multicultural curriculum to life in your own classroom.

## Transformation of Society

Ultimately, the goal of multicultural education is to contribute to the positive transformation of society and to the negotiation and maintenance of social justice and equity. This stands to reason, as the transformation of schools will necessarily transform a society that puts so much stock in educational attainment, academic degrees, and test scores. In fact, it is exactly this competitive stance so prevalent in the United States (and increasingly the world, with American "help") that multicultural education aims to challenge, shake, expose, and critique.

By employing traditional curricula and ways of teaching, schools continually provide privilege to the privileged and ongoing struggle to the struggling with very little hope of transformation. By this I mean that those who have historically succeeded in our schools (mostly White middle-class children) continue to succeed and those who have been failed by schooling continue to be pushed out (for example, children of color and/or low-income families [Derman-Sparks & Ramsey, 2011; Goodwin & Genor, 2008]). "Informal" tracking, standardized testing, discrepancies in the quality of schools within and across regions, and other inequitable practices remain. These have historically shaped schooling—even before school integration—and continue to do so today.

To promote change and create equitable learning communities, teachers can engage in advancing multicultural teaching and learning principles both inside and out of the classroom (Nieto, 2003). We cannot equate the perception that the vast majority of schools are "well-intentioned" with the assumption that schools are immune to the inequities of society. They are not. As multicultural educators, as teachers who believe and are invested in equity, we are committed to ask unaskable questions. We explore and question structures of power and privilege that maintain inequities within our own classrooms and beyond. But when and how do we start?

## A CRITICAL APPROACH TO
## MULTICULTURAL CURRICULUM AND TEACHING

Multicultural education is about equity—and in the early childhood classroom, equity has to do with whose voices are heard and read. It is about creating opportunities for "all students [to] acquire the knowledge, attitudes, and skills needed to participate in cross-cultural interactions and in personal, social, and civic action that will help make our nation more democratic and just" (Banks, 2007, p. xii). It is about developing these knowledges, attitudes, and skills as a teacher as well. But how? There are many ways of teaching multiculturally—some of which are explored throughout this book; some of which I hope will be developed in your own classroom. This book is based on the simple premise that multicultural teaching is good teaching for *all* children. After all, multicultural education brings to life the nation's commitment to democracy, freedom, equality, and justice (Gay, 1994). As you will learn by reading the following chapters in this book, even in light of standardized curriculum guides, there are ways of bringing multicultural education to life in most (pre)schools and classrooms, striving toward educational excellence for all.

As educators committed to equity and excellence, we often talk about what multicultural education is, why it is needed. We read about it. We write about it. Much of the literature on multicultural education reminds us that *what is* in classrooms and (pre)schools must change in order to pursue ways of teaching that value and honor the humanity of each and every child—honoring them as social, cultural, and historical beings. This literature proposes that change is possible. However, seldom in reading this literature do we learn *how* this change might take place (Hoffman, 1996; Sleeter & Bernal, 2003). This book shows insights into how this change *is occurring* in a variety of early childhood classrooms, featuring teachers who engage in critical multicultural education day in and day out. In child-focused and centered ways, they instill in children the awareness of their ability to change unfair and unjust relationships. Young children then come to envision and embrace the necessity to promote positive change.

The teachers featured in this book illustrate their belief that in order to engage in critical multicultural education, it is important to prioritize children's personal, practical knowledge as foundational. To do so, they propose that it is imperative to listen to children and value what they say. Through their practices, these teachers openly acknowledge that there are culturally situated ways of learning and that there may be multiple discontinuities or mismatches between home and school, or between one's home culture and the culture of school (Moll, Amanti, Neff, & González, 1992). Yet, in their teaching and learning, they draw on the practices in which individual children and their families engage, honoring culturally specific ways of communicating and experiencing the world. Their practices illustrate Nieto's belief: "Culture does not exist in a vacuum but rather is situated in particular historical, social, political, and economic conditions" (2002, p. 11).

Over the last 3 decades, many researchers have documented diverse cultural identities in classrooms, homes, and communities across the country (Cazden, 1986; Heath, 1983; Valdés, 1996). Their studies can contribute to our knowledge base, allowing us to recognize the need to learn more about the cultures of the children we teach as opposed to measuring them against our own primary cultural practices. Such studies remind us that if we are going to engage in critical multicultural education, we need to pay attention to the individual experiences of the children we teach as opposed to drawing on stereotypes and large generalizations of groups to which they may belong—as no two African American families are the same, and even within a family, no two children are the same. Thus, recognizing the similarities and differences that human beings embody while engaging in learning about the specific children we teach, we need to move beyond the "heroes and holidays" approach to multicultural education, so problematic yet so prevalent in (pre)schools throughout the country (Lee, Menkart, & Okazawa-Rey, 2002). As I consider issues of race, culture, gender, socioeconomics, sexuality, power, and (in)equities in a variety of classrooms, I do so from a critical perspective that seeks to problematize what is, envisioning what could be, creating a more hopeful future while acknowledging the constraints of an unjust educational system.

To teach multiculturally means to teach inclusively, to create spaces of possibility, to bring differences front and center in the life of the classroom. This involves positioning power at the center of our teaching. After all, it is not possible to engage with race and gender or to question structures of privilege unless we consider power relations. As with any approach to teaching, there are shortcomings in multicultural education and culturally responsive pedagogy given that they are both examples of "the cultural difference paradigm" (Goodwin, Cheruvu, & Genishi, 2008, p. 5) and that the "cultural difference movement is not entirely free of assumptions of the deficit and inferiority approaches" (p. 5).

## STUDENTS AND TEACHERS AS CULTURAL BEINGS

The first step toward change is the critical awareness of and reflection on one's cultural location—as teachers and as children who are distinct members of classroom communities. While histories shape individuals, through questioning and problematizing, through enacting change, individuals can (re)shape their own histories as they consider their past, live the present, and redirect their future. Power and identity are always socially negotiated constructs—and can be placed at the center of the critical multicultural early childhood classroom.

The connection between practical strategies and issues of power lies with teachers, which is why the continual critical examination of and reflection on self is so important. To engage in this kind of work, we must be ready to acknowledge the ways we are (and have been) privileged and be prepared to change our mindsets. Again, I invite you to examine your beliefs and reconceptualize your own stances toward diversities. While I acknowledge that such reconceptualizing is complex, time consuming, and a long-term project involving critical and often political perspectives about self (Goodwin & Genor, 2008; Oakes & Lipton, 1999), I believe that in order to engage in multicultural education, we early childhood educators need to engage in reflection and question our own stances as an ongoing part of our personal and professional lives.

### Questioning Privileges and Identities

Derman-Sparks and Edwards (2010) proposed that anti-bias education goals must foster, for all children,

- Self-awareness, confidence, family pride, and positive social identities
- Comfort and joy with human diversity, and accurate language for human differences
- Deep, caring human connections
- Recognition of fairness, language to describe unfairness, and understanding that unfairness hurts
- Empowerment and the skills to act against prejudice and/or discrimination—collectively or individually

The approaches, strategies, and tools presented in this book are situated representations of this kind of anti-bias, multicultural teaching. Yet, here, I propose that these goals apply to teachers as well. After all, a prerequisite to seeing all children as worthy human beings is to acknowledge that we are each worthy cultural beings, to acknowledge that we see the world culturally, and to trouble our beliefs and assumptions. The identities that we occupy—in terms of race, gender, class, sexuality, language, or ability—position us in certain ways, thus affording us certain privileges or conferring deficit-ridden stereotypes.

As I ask you to consider your privileges and identities, I reveal mine, acknowledging that they position me in ways that are both oppressive and empowering. I am a Latina woman of mixed race, heterosexual, able-bodied, a primary speaker of Portuguese who holds a Ph.D. from an American public university. I am a mother of two sons. I am married to a White man. I enjoy what I do professionally, and my family income has allowed me to pay for quality early care for both of my children. I had the opportunity to teach children from preschool to 2nd grade in the United States and in Brazil.

Yet, I did not benefit from the economic, educational, and political advantages of being White. I still get asked if I am my own children's babysitter—by students in their school and by adults who want to hire a well-educated Latina nanny. They ask, "I heard you go to Columbia. How much do you charge?" After hearing questions such as this multiple times, I am aware that I answer with a certain (and troublesome) normalcy that I am their mother, and at times I reply that I am a professor at Teachers College, Columbia University. Often, my accented English positions me as uneducated despite my Ph.D. I repeatedly get yelled at during phone calls since those unfamiliar with me tend to think that my accent communicates a lack of understanding or limited hearing and that yelling will somehow enhance communication.

I have layers of privilege and resistance, though. Prior to immigrating to the United States, I attended a progressive, democratic, non-profit school co-founded by Paulo Freire—the school operated (and still does) according to his educational philosophy. I was involved in unions and in political movements. I was an activist. I was born in Recife, Brazil, to a family of activists who believed in life and education as political endeavors. I was inspired by my father who took part in anti-dictatorship movements in Brazil and risked his own freedom many times in the name of democracy. Today, I am financially able to live in Manhattan. I am "documented" and able to safely travel within and across countries. I am able to communicate with others in three languages. I am privileged to have the career that I do—to have the support of my family and of close friends. Despite stereotypes which frame me every day—mostly based on race, ethnicity, language, and gender—I am privileged and feel that I can author my own life.

I do not offer this account of who I am as a warning that White teachers cannot engage in equitable teaching. I believe that all teachers have the potential and responsibility to teach multiculturally. Ladson-Billings (1994) documented the successful practices of eight teachers of African American children (three of whom were White). And some prominent anti-bias early educators are White—Louise Derman-Sparks and Patricia Ramsey. (I recommend their book *What If All the Kids Are White?: Anti-Bias Multicultural Education with Young Children and Families* [2011], as a wonderful companion to this book.) So, regardless of how you identify yourself, before proceeding to the following chapters, I ask you to consider the following questions:

- Who am I as a cultural being?
- What cultural threads make up the fabric of who I am?
- What aspects of my identity afford me privileges?
- What are the racial and linguistic backgrounds of those who surround me in school/at work? What does this tell me?
- What assumptions do outsiders associate with me? What do these assumptions tell me about the privileges and oppressions I experience?
- Do I see and actively question inequities that exist in the (pre) schools where I work?

These are seemingly simple, yet important questions to consider.

If you are White (as are 78% of teachers of young children—Saluja, Early, & Clifford, 2002), the first step is to recognize that as a White person, you too are a cultural being. Perhaps you may have been thinking that you were just "normal." But unless we challenge this idea of *White = Normal*, we will continue imposing Whiteness as the standard against which all others are scaled and rated. It is imperative to recognize "the ideological mechanisms that shape and maintain our racist order" (Bartolomé & Macedo, 1997, p. 223). To do so, it is essential to become aware of and to problematize society's "deeply rooted assumptions that schools are inherently fair, that children's capacities to learn are predetermined and unalterable, and that meritocratic competition is the route to equal educational opportunity" (Goodwin & Genor, 2008, p. 201). We must acknowledge and trouble as pervasive inequities that

> too many children of color, poor children, or children who are new immigrants continue to experience troubled and limiting school lives. As a society, we have come to accept too easily as "business as usual" what should stand out as stark aberrations and deep contradictions: race and socioeconomic status as "predictors" of poor school performance; gifted classrooms that exclude most children of color; "minorities" and the poor always doing less well on standardized tests than those in the white middle class; children of color disproportionately labeled as behavior problems and assigned to special education; and schools serving culturally and linguistically diverse children invariably being resource poor. (pp. 214–215)

With this book, I want to interrupt this racist and/or privileged way of seeing the world, this ideology of inequity—and invite you to engage in self-reflection and analysis so that you can come to more clearly see all the inequities and injustices in (pre)schools and classrooms today. While this is not easy work, it is necessary as the vast majority of today's teachers are White females who come from middle-class, monolingual backgrounds (Cochran-Smith, 2004) and by the next census in 2020, White children are projected to become the minority in America's (pre)schools (Frey, 2011).

## Examining Beliefs About Education

Your beliefs regarding education are culturally shaped and based on your past experiences—of privilege and oppression. Unless you trouble such privileges and oppressions, you are likely to make decisions regarding teaching that will maintain the status quo—what is will continue. It is fine if you have not had extensive experiences with those who are different from you—but it is important to acknowledge this fact and to learn that your unspoken values and cultural knowledge are partial to your experiences. Thus, it is important to recognize your own self as a cultural, historical, and social being. After all, reading about critical multicultural education will do little if you do not engage in documenting what you see, reflecting on your own privileges, and acting to change your beliefs and practices.

We each come to teaching with preconceived notions about education, about ourselves, and about others—and these notions need to be troubled and examined. As suggested by Goodwin and Genor (2008), I invite you to engage in reflection and consider writing an autobiography in which you explore who you are as a historical and cultural being and the possible impact your experiences may have on the way you teach—on your actions, priorities, and choices. I want you to disrupt your ideologies and comfort zones by recognizing that the way you view students is informed by the beliefs and preconceived notions you had before you ever met them.

As you do so, I hope that you can counter your own assumptions as you step outside of yourself—not allowing your previous assumptions and experiences to limit your vision and actions of who you will be as a teacher and how you will teach. I hope that you will teach in ways that are different from your own school experiences—addressing any gaps or issues that you now see in your own education. Most of all, I hope that as you analyze who you are and who you want to be—as a teacher and human being—you come to interrupt inequities and confront assumptions that have gone unquestioned. I hope that your cultural locations can become sites of "interruption," lenses you can utilize to critically examine how your lived cultural experiences mediate your ways of knowing the world, the ways that schools structure inequality, and the ways in which you can make a firm and deliberate commitment to multicultural education, social justice, and social change.

## AN INVITATION:
## CAREFULLY CONSIDERING APPROACHES, STRATEGIES, AND TOOLS

This book showcases early childhood teachers who have brought multicultural education to life in their classrooms, moving beyond "heroes and holidays." I sincerely hope that their practices offer insights and shed light onto possibilities for you to engage in multicultural education in your own classroom or (pre)school. They not only show what is possible, but highlight the urgency of engaging in and promoting education that is more equitable, culturally responsive, and inclusive. This kind of teaching blurs the role of teacher and learner, positioning students as experts from whom much can (and should) be learned. It also blurs the boundaries of school, homes, and communities, as it takes an expansive approach to learning that is grounded in true community connections and partnerships. This kind of learning with young children illustrates multiple paths to diverse solutions for culturally and linguistically complex classrooms in which teachers move systematically toward multicultural ends—communicating high expectations, genuine care, and true love.

As you read the forthcoming chapters, I invite you to consider the approaches, tools, and strategies employed by the featured early childhood teachers. As you enter Head Start, preschool, kindergarten, 1st-, and 2nd-grade classrooms, I hope that you will learn from the children and their teachers. These chapters are not meant to give you a step-by-step list of what to do, but to shed light onto the possibilities, approaches, strategies, and tools available, as you get started with or enhance your multicultural teaching. As you read them, I invite you to think about your own classrooms, (pre)schools, situations, contexts, and identities as you consider a number of possible ways of teaching multiculturally. I hope that these narratives speak to you and that they inform and connect to your everyday life and practices as a teacher in relevant ways.

These chapters portray a variety of voices and perspectives. There are similarities in the ways that the teachers forge relationships with the children they teach and in their intentional listening to children's voices. Nevertheless, there are differences. Each of the strategies and tools portrayed in this book is aligned with the aims of critical multicultural education—they all seek to foster anti-bias, social justice–focused education. Yet, instead of proposing one single approach to teaching multiculturally in the early years, I believe that it is important to present a variety of diverse approaches. The commitment to teach equitably crosses approaches and strategies, remaining constant throughout the book. So does the honoring of children's histories, stories, identities, and voices. However, the sampling of teaching approaches, tools, and strategies presented here illustrates that there are many valid ways to teach multiculturally.

You are about to embark on an exciting journey through a variety of early childhood classrooms. The upcoming chapters contain powerful stories, explanations, examples, and dimensions that will help you understand, adapt, and reinvent multicultural approaches in your own context, in your own classroom. Ready? I hope so. After all, "it is on all our close, small classroom stages where universal human rights—social justice—can begin" (Genishi & Goodwin, 2008, p. 278).

# CHAPTER 3

# Interviews: Encouraging Children to Ask Questions

Why? When? Why? Enter an early childhood classroom and you are prone to hear many questions being asked. Young children ask questions all the time. They want to know why there are stars in the sky, when they will be able to play outside, why they have to clean up, when they will have a turn, and why another child is laughing (or crying). While we adults tend to answer children's questions, we may also discourage them from asking questions. "Stop asking so many questions" comes out of adults' mouths too often—and results in children's questions being pushed aside, diminished, and finally disappearing altogether. This may happen because some adults feel inadequate at answering questions they don't have a clear and easy answer to. In the early childhood classroom, it may happen because these questions appear to detract from learning. So, by the time children enter the elementary grades, they may stop asking questions. Yet, I would like you to think about the possibilities of inviting children to continue asking questions—even those we don't know how to or want to answer; even those questions apparently unconnected to the curriculum. I invite you to consider *interviews* as a way to genuinely build on the strengths of young children—by encouraging them to continue asking: Why? When? Why?

Interviews are not usually associated with the early childhood curriculum. Yet, asking focused or big questions of community members who are experts in specific areas, and learning from their answers, can be placed at the center of the curriculum, becoming major sources of new information and fostering active learning in early childhood classrooms. Interviews tap into the expertise existent beyond the classroom walls while at the same time making community members relatable (children may have things in common with the person being interviewed) and real to young children. They can be starting points for an exploratory learning journey, expanding teaching and learning in multicultural ways—or they can be ways to add perspectives to those already present in the early childhood learning community.

In addition to making educational experiences more equitable and contributing to fashioning a more complete curriculum, placing interviews at the center of learning applies to anything and everything. Inviting children to learn more about a topic by asking questions of community and family members is inviting children to become researchers and to learn from the everyday stories people tell. In addition, interviewing allows children to examine society along with its greatness and its unfair practices in a meaningful and genuine way—in a way that makes sense to them as young children. Asking questions is about searching for answers, about researching. Young children are already researchers—they always ask questions and want to find out new things. Interviewing thus invites children to research, collect information, and analyze the world in which they live.

## WHY INTERVIEWS AS A STRATEGY FOR TEACHING MULTICULTURALLY?

Interviews are a way to make teaching and learning richer—and fairer. They allow us to move away from teaching Eurocentric curricula that have for so long been honored in early childhood classrooms throughout the country. Especially in early childhood education, historically there has been a deficit approach to diversities—which frames diverse children and their families as biologically and/or culturally inferior (Goodwin, Cheruvu, & Genishi, 2008; Valdés, 1996). A Eurocentric curriculum continues to reinforce these perceptions. Instead of relying on single accounts of events or understandings of the world that position White, middle-class, Mainstream American English–speaking children as normal, interviews can expand what we teach and learn in early childhood classrooms—and make learning more engaging, relevant, and real. Such learning recognizes that children, their families, and their communities have rich cultural practices and precious histories—and builds upon these. As a result, *all* children come to a fuller understanding of the world in which they live.

Interviews not only expand what is being taught and learned, but allow students to develop more nuanced and fuller understandings of issues affecting the local and global communities in which they live. Through interviews, children can come to see their families and communities in a more positive and worthy light, thereby challenging the idea that diverse children (and families and communities) are deficient or inferior. By positioning family and community bodies of knowledge at the center of learning, we can engage in honoring children's backgrounds and building on their strengths. As they listen closely to family and community members, children come to critically read the world in which they live, questioning inequities.

Students can then use their knowledge to bring about social action (Oyler, 2011). This social action—which must be relevant to the children—may involve talking with community members and stakeholders, writing letters to politicians, expanding the school's library holdings, and bringing awareness to an issue in a variety of ways. Thus, through interviews, children can come to identify an issue, ask questions about that issue, consider a variety of perspectives and points of view, value firsthand knowledge, problematize what is, and start moving toward positive change, fostering (even if in small ways) what could be. For example, change may be as small as adding books to library holdings that are more representative of the races and languages represented in the school.

When interviews are a central focus of teaching and learning, they become major sources of new information and concepts. Interviews create the time and space for understanding and appreciating oneself and others. Sometimes an interview may serve as an introduction to one's own cultural background. I have found that because some cultures and languages are marginalized in society, parents may not engage in meaningful conversations with their children about their family's histories and cultural practices. Bringing such knowledge to the center of the curriculum not only expands the curriculum being taught, but contributes to children better understanding and embracing their identities, resulting in improved self-esteem. Interviewing a family member—bringing this person into the spotlight of a particular classroom, of a particular community of learners—can shift how a child views that person (Rogovin, 1998). In addition, as children listen to a variety of perspectives, points of view, experiences, and knowledges, they come to appreciate and respect the unique experiences of their families and may move from feeling ashamed to feeling proud.

Interviews can expand the curriculum, making it more multicultural. Many times the concepts and information learned through interviews are not available in published books—and even when they are, they are not as real and relatable as they are in interviews. Interviews are a way to be fully inclusive and to value bodies of knowledge that have been traditionally marginalized. And interviews unfold right in front of the children and the teacher(s). The children are active members of the interview—they design and ask questions, they engage in discussion, take notes, etc. Interviews are thus a very engaging and active form of learning. Interviews can be a starting point for a learning journey—or they can be culminations in the search for answering big questions. And interviews are interconnected to the curriculum—to reading, writing, science, math, and the arts—or at least they can be. Interviews can be a way of getting started or a way to expand learning in early childhood settings. But—how?

## WAYS TO USE INTERVIEWS

Interviews do not emerge from a vacuum. They can be linked to students' interests, to curriculum objectives—or both at the same time. They may start from students' backgrounds and histories—who they are as social, cultural, and historical beings. As we bring someone to the classroom or go out to the community, we become learner-teachers and teacher-learners. Teachers and students become researchers together. They ask real questions. They seek answers. They come to understand topics in multidimensional and multicultural ways. Interviews comprise a powerful and malleable way of engaging in multicultural teaching—they can define the teaching and learning of a classroom community or serve to add depth and breadth to its learning journey. Thus, interviews can be used as strategies shaping an immersion approach or as tools enriching an inquiry-based curriculum.

Interviews may be part of an immersion approach—"whatever your theme of study, immerse yourself and your class in it, live it, breathe it" (Rogovin, 1998, p. xv). In New York City, regardless of the theme being studied, 1st-grade teacher Paula Rogovin (1998) sees a place for immersing oneself in learning through interviews. Instead of learning solely from books or online sources, she invites the children to value firsthand accounts, bringing them to the center of the curriculum. In this way, classroom and community become one, and children become boundary crossers and world learners. After all, this approach allows students to start with the stories and histories which are often absent from the official curriculum, but that are very relevant in their lives.

In Mary Cowhey's 2nd-grade class in Northampton, Massachusetts, interviewees are invited to the classroom to help children answer a "big question." In doing this, Ms. Cowhey positions herself vulnerably—as she admits that she does not know the answers to all questions being asked. This stance opens up possibilities for children to respect each other regardless of previous experiences or abilities. In truly pursuing these questions, she moves away from the all-too-common, guess-what-I-am-thinking kind of questions, which seek to assess students' knowledge. Interviews enter the curriculum in authentic ways—as a function of children's genuine curiosity and inquiry.

As you read this chapter, I invite you to think about the many ways that interviews can be employed in your own early childhood classroom. I hope that you will reinvent interviews in ways that expand the curriculum and teaching of your classroom and in ways that lead to authentic and meaningful family engagement.

## GETTING STARTED

There are no formulas for using interviews as tools for multicultural education. Nevertheless, it is important to assure that those interviewed contribute a variety of perspectives to the learning experience. The topics of study, the children you are teaching, the families that make up your classroom community, as well as the resources available will determine how interviews come to life. And when you position interviews at the center of your teaching and learning, you may find that they come to life differently from year to year. It is important to recognize that it takes time to fully develop the potential of interviews as tools for learning multiculturally. As you incorporate interviews into your teaching, you will become more skilled and develop more effective strategies—and so will the children you teach. It may take time to become skilled at identifying how the content of interviews may meet curricular goals, objectives, and standards. But it is possible. Yet, it is important—and I would venture to say easy—to get started.

An interview approach to teaching and learning is multicultural—or has the potential to be. It is about finding out more about the world—especially those experiences and aspects that are not as well known. It is detective work. It necessitates recognizing what children know, what they bring to the classroom, and who they are as cultural beings. So, start asking questions—meaningful and real questions which will result in learning. As a teacher, this involves embracing the unknown. And while the unknown can be scary, to truly engage in multicultural education, the roles of teacher and learner must be blurred. After all, no teacher knows it all; no student knows it all—nor is anyone ignorant of everything (Freire, 1998). Together teachers and students can ask questions and engage in an exciting learning journey.

## Develop Resources

In seeking to address questions, teacher(s) and students think of new ways they may be able to pursue answers (or at least access new information). Then, they may invite guests who will offer additional perspectives and enrich the understandings of the classroom community. In terms of the resources available, there is much that can be discovered if we learn about and forge relationships with the families that make up our classrooms. Classroom families can serve as your primary partners as you seek to identify interviewees—they may serve as interviewees themselves or may facilitate connections with individuals they know. If the classroom community has questions that cannot be answered by family members—through family interviews—or if the classroom community is not very diverse, as a teacher and member of the school community, you can reach beyond your class so that students can interview those who are part of the broader school community—such as other teachers, paraprofessionals, custodians, and families of children in other classrooms.

To get to know and gather information about the families of her students, Paula Rogovin (1998) sends home surveys at the beginning of the school year. Mary Cowhey engages in home visits where she gets to know families and family members as unique human beings. She says,

I don't go with a big agenda. I go to learn the names and faces of my students and the people who love them. I go to listen and answer questions if the student and family have any. I learn hundreds of valuable things about my students and their families, easily and sometimes even wordlessly, that will help me connect with and teach them in culturally relevant ways. Most important, I establish a partnership with the parents and guardians and begin to forge a commitment to work together to teach their children.

During those home visits, in addition to forging authentic relationships with the families of the children she will teach, Mary Cowhey takes note of the family members' experiences, work, and general funds of knowledge. She then draws on this database of resident experts who are part of the classroom family as she thinks about teaching and learning in authentic ways. Depending on the topic, it may be necessary to reach out to people outside of the classroom and school—but even then your classroom families may be of help in identifying potential interviewees or making arrangements. As you communicate with the families of the children in your classroom and with your colleagues, you will likely have dozens of adults looking for people to be interviewed by your class. This becomes a true community effort.

## Compose Questions

Prior to an interview, members of the classroom community need to compose important questions to ask—thus learning to focus. This comes after the big question or topic has been defined. When children offer questions, I invite you to write them on chart paper so that they are easily visualized and can be revised as the children see fit. They rehearse interview questions, revise, and rehearse some more. Teachers may also have questions, and as full members of the classroom community, can ask them. Teachers' questions may reflect curriculum requirements or their particular concerns and curiosities regarding the topic being addressed. During the interview, the teacher may serve as a recorder (as in Ms. Cowhey's classroom) and/or children may be invited to record their observations in interview journals (as in Ms. Rogovin's classroom). Paula Rogovin (1998) underscores the importance of encouraging students to take note of interview learnings in ways that make sense to them—through art notes or invented spelling. Mary Cowhey emphasizes the importance of recording exactly what is being said and how it is being said—without any corrections or interpretations. In addition, an audio or video recording can be made and later reviewed with the children—this may become a valuable source if questions arise as to what the interviewee said.

## Reflect on Learning

After interviews, the community of learners can reflect on their learning. This is a powerful space for challenging and debunking stereotypes. For example, children who may have gendered associations about ballet can come to revisit and revise their assumption and gendered stereotype upon interviewing a male ballet dancer; children who may assume scientists are men can have their assumption challenged through an interview with a woman scientist.

Yet, in conducting interviews, it is important to take into consideration children's attitudes—especially if they are overtly or covertly insensitive or hostile to people of specific nationalities, races, languages, abilities, etc. Thus, I invite you not only to plan your interviews based on children's big questions or on curriculum goals, objectives, and standards, but to select interviewees who will raise the issues which are at the center of prejudice and stereotypes in the classroom. This may be done through inviting adults of diverse races, religions, and nationalities to be interviewed. Furthermore, exploring and refuting stereotypes can be done by selecting a passage of the interview to be revisited during a later discussion, placing special focus on the issue raised—for example, all Asians not being great at math (Chang & Au, 2008) and all Latinos not being underemployed.

## Use New Information

Because interviews are such relatable and active learning experiences, learnings from interviews often become topics of conversation on the playground and at the family dinner table. Children voluntarily share what they learned because they are excited about those interviews. Children may share ways that they are similar to and different from the person being interviewed and share changes in their beliefs following interviews. Thus, family members become involved in the learning process, many times suggesting and arranging subsequent interviews or coming to be interviewed themselves.

Finally, children may use the information they learned to help improve their worlds. So, not only do children develop a fuller understanding of the worlds in which they live, but they also act upon their learnings and seek to rewrite their communities and societies in more hopeful ways, even if in small steps. Some of these attempts at rewriting their worlds have to do with fostering more equity—through promoting awareness in their school community, writing letters to politicians and stakeholders, or marching to demand justice.

## CONSIDERING OBSTACLES, EXPLORING POSSIBILITIES

Interviews offer a variety of teaching and learning possibilities. Yet, it is important to consider some of the obstacles to bringing such a teaching approach to life as we explore possibilities. I invite you to stop and think about some of the obstacles and possibilities of employing interviews as a strategy for teaching multiculturally.

One of the possible obstacles may have to do with *the location of a school.* It is likely that a class in New York City (such as Paula Rogovin's) may have an easier time locating a ballet dancer than a class in rural Wyoming. Yet, now with Internet-mediated video calls, these barriers can be broken. Still, I want to underscore the power of having a real person who lives in the community come to the classroom if possible. After all, as Rogovin (1998) wrote: "People are our primary source of information. They know their cultures, their occupations, their histories in ways most books cannot convey" (p. 43).

You may not speak *the first language of the interviewee.* If you feel that this is an obstacle, it is an easy fix: Recruit someone to translate. A family or community member may be available. The key here is not to exclude family or community members based on their language. While a bit more challenging to orchestrate, repositioning the language expectations and practices of the classroom and valuing students whose home languages do not coincide with the language privileged in school may prove to be an invaluable experience.

Another possible obstacle may be that of *a standardized curriculum.* How do you engage in interviews when you have a curriculum to follow—or even a guide that paces what you need to teach each day? You do not need to have the entire day dedicated to interviewing. An interview will typically take no more than 30 or 40 minutes in an early childhood setting. So, instead of thinking about interviews as a whole-day, whole-week, whole-year affair, you can think about a 30- to 40-minute investment to expand the curriculum. Then, as you are teaching your standardized curriculum, you can make teaching and learning more responsive to *all* children by including interviews. Interviews can easily address the areas of oral language development and writing workshop (learning how to write focused questions in the primary grades). I suggest that you look closely at your schedule and find some wiggle room—30–40 minutes for a classroom interview. If you can find this time, you have addressed a big obstacle.

Yet another obstacle may be that of *meeting the standards.* I've heard the following question before: "How am I supposed to meet all the standards? I just don't have time for these interviews." Well—interviews can and do address many of the curriculum standards for your particular grade and likely for more advanced grades. You will need to know the standards well in order to make connections between what your interview is addressing and what the standards mandate. I believe that as you engage in this exercise, you will find that interviews address many more standards than you initially thought. Also—as long as your questions are authentic—do not hesitate to ask questions that allow an interviewee to delve further into learning that is related to standards. And—make learning visible. If you are in an educational setting where colleagues and administrators are not as confident in the power of interviews, make a clear display that connects the interview learning to standards. You will then be able to negotiate even more wiggle room in your schedule—and perhaps even sway other teachers to try interviews in their classrooms too.

One other obstacle may simply be *scheduling the interview*—especially if there are many transitions during the school day, if you are teaching in a half-day program, or if you are a pull-out or early intervention teacher. Again—think 30–40 minutes. You may want to try conducting the interview at the beginning of the day. But minimizing transitions is essential. In addition, it is necessary to accommodate the schedule of the person being interviewed. Finally, think about this as a unique learning opportunity and as an event that will not take place on a daily (and likely not even on a weekly) basis.

Interviews allow us to teach more authentically, responsively, and multiculturally. Interviews allow us to truly engage families in ways that honor their funds of knowledge and in ways that matter to the learning experience of the classroom community. Through interviews, students can develop a greater awareness of the world, as they consider many perspectives and points of view. According to Mary Cowhey, they come to ask questions such as "Where's your evidence?" as opposed to accepting accounts at face value. Students can then move beyond their individual selves and collectively seek to promote change.

## ENACTING INTERVIEWS IN AN EARLY CHILDHOOD SETTING

What does an early childhood classroom look like when a teacher uses interviews to teach multiculturally? While there are many ways to bring interviews to life in early childhood classrooms, here I invite you to listen closely to Mary Cowhey and learn how interviews came to life in her 2nd grade. Let's begin by learning about the teacher and the school where she teaches.

### The Teacher

Mary Cowhey has been teaching primary grades for 15 years at Jackson Street School, a public elementary school in Northampton, Massachusetts. She is from a family of teachers. Prior to being a teacher, she was a community organizer and activist for 14 years. She became interested in teaching because it was a way to make positive social change. She thought that teaching would be a way to promote change one child, one class at a time—and then the changes would ripple out to the children's families, communities, and futures. She entered teaching with a commitment to change, already seeing teaching as a political act. She was in her 30s when she entered the initial teacher certification program and brought a very critical perspective to her education. She questioned and problematized what was being presented in teacher preparation classes—which at times resulted in attempts to silence her. This strengthened her commitment to teach in urban settings. Writing in her own voice, Mary Cowhey describes and analyzes her teaching in the next two sections.

## The Classroom

Welcome to Jackson Street School, where I teach. Jackson Street is one of four elementary schools in Northampton, MA. It houses the district's English language learning, alternative learning, and autism programs, and has the most diverse student population in the district. Demographically, the school has around 300 students, of which 56% are White, 25% are Latino/a, 6% are Asian/Asian American, 4% are African American, 1% is Native American, and 8% are multiracial; 19% of students are English language learners; 20% have identified special needs; and 45% qualify for free and/or reduced lunch. According to the Massachusetts Department of Education, half of the school's families are classified as low-income.

I use philosophical discussions to create a habit of critical inquiry in the classroom. People often ask me how I get children to ask such great questions. While you cannot force children to ask what we adults would call great questions, you can create an environment where big questions are encouraged and valued.

Entering my first science class in college at the age of 36, 20 years after I'd last taken a science class in high school, I was feeling very inadequate. When the professor began the course by saying that whatever scientific knowledge we brought into the classroom that day didn't matter as much as our ability to ask good questions, my anxiety washed away. My confidence soared, as I thought, "I can do this. I have been annoying and provoking people with questions my whole life!"

At the beginning of every year I tell my students that story to shake up the misconception that has already taken root by the age of 7, that asking questions means you're dumb. I tell them I like questions, because they show me that students are engaged and thinking critically, and that I love big questions. My short definition of a big question is one that takes more than 5 minutes to answer adequately. Big questions are the ones that make you stop short, the ones that take your breath away with their depth or implications. In my classroom, I am like a primitive hunter-gatherer, ever on the prowl for a big question. For me, the most important thing is to listen—a challenge for a talkative person like me. To capture those big questions, I can't be the one talking all the time. I have to create rich discussions when the children are talking with each other, so I can listen. That's what got me interested in doing philosophy with children.

In class I read rich, authentic children's literature and then open a philosophical discussion in which students and teacher ask and respond to open-ended questions. First, I clarify my expectations for how to participate in a philosophical discussion—that there are no right and wrong answers, that everyone's voice is welcomed and encouraged. The first time I tried this with my 1st- and 2nd-graders, a student responded to the first question. Just then, a 1st-grader burst out in tears, sobbing, "That's what I was gonna say. He stole the idea right outta my head!" I sat there, stunned and open-mouthed, realizing the weakness of my adult logic, thinking, "No one can reach in your head and steal your idea. . . ." Instead of arguing with an emotional 6-year-old, I decided to go with empathy. "Isn't it frustrating when someone says the good idea you were about to say?" The sobbing 1st-grader sniffled and nodded, then glared across the circle at the Idea Thief. I continued, "We could feel angry and upset, or we could feel happy that someone else had the same good idea we did. The next time this happens, I'd like you to try this. Take a deep breath, raise your hand and say, 'I agree with Ben.' Then you could build on his idea to make it both of yours, by giving an example from the story or from real life. We can call this 'agree and extend.'" We rehearsed how to do that. We also discussed the possibility that someone might have an idea that someone else strongly disagrees with and that it would be inappropriate to say something like, "That's a stupid idea." We practiced how to respectfully disagree and pose a counterexample, citing evidence from the text or illustration or an example from real life.

Every year I read my students the *Frog and Toad Together* (Lobel, 1971) story, "Dragons and Giants," and engage in a philosophical discussion about the nature of bravery. After Frog and Toad read stories about brave characters who stood up to dragons and giants, they wonder whether they are brave. Frog and Toad challenge themselves to climb a mountain, where they encounter an avalanche, a snake, and a hawk. While the story explores the complex concept of bravery, it is funny to children because Frog and Toad become very scared when they encounter scary things—they tremble, their bodies and voices shake, and they cry out, but they continue to climb the mountain. Eventually Frog and Toad run all the way home and hide—one under the covers and one in the closet. The story ends with Frog and Toad each saying they are glad to have such a brave friend.

One year, after reading the story, I asked, "Is there anyone who is brave all the time?" So the children started trying to answer this question. One boy said his uncle's pit bulls were brave all the time, because they barked at everyone. Another student said that professional wrestlers were brave all the time, but another child (whose family had recently been in a car accident) disagreed and posed a counterexample, saying that if the professional wrestler got in a car accident, he would be scared. One child brought up Gandhi's Salt March to the Sea and said that Gandhi was always brave. Another child disagreed, saying, "No, remember in that book about Gandhi, when he got married, his wife used to tease him because he was afraid to sleep with the light off. So, even Gandhi would get scared." The children continued going back and forth, creating an energetic learning buzz, until one of the children said: "God. I think God would never get scared." This comment silenced the members of the classroom community.

My students are spiritually diverse: Jewish, Pentecostal, Muslim, atheist, Catholic, Unitarian, Buddhist, Hindu, and more. After a brief moment of silence, the children began to discuss their ideas of God, mostly agreeing that God would not be scared. Until one boy said, "But, wait a minute. Just imagine if you were God and then something really, really bad happened, like Hurricane Katrina, and there were floods, and like you saw all your little people, and they were, you know, in this bad flood, and you couldn't stop it." So, the children considered this image of a worried God who couldn't stop Hurricane Katrina—a very parental image of God, who couldn't save all his children. This really got all the children's attention.

Then one girl said: "Wait a minute, wait a minute. What about God's baby?" "That's Jesus, he wouldn't be scared," another child said. The girl continued: "But Jesus was a baby; and what baby, if that baby gotta get shots, ain't gonna cry? Imagine baby Jesus. And the nurse give him a shot. Well, baby Jesus gonna cry! Cuz all babies cry. All babies scared of shots. No baby ain't gonna cry when they get a shot, you know."

Then another boy asked: "Ms. Cowhey, do you know all the stories in the Bible?" I responded, "Well, I know some stories in the Bible, but I don't know all of them." He persisted, "Does anyone know all the stories in the Bible?" After a brief silence, I answered, "Oh yes, there are people who study religion and they would. Pastors and rabbis and priests—they would know all the stories in the Bible." His response was, "Do you think if we could find somebody who read all the stories in the Bible, we could ask them if God ever got scared?"

This was an interesting question, a big question. Since no one in the class thought that anyone in their family had read all the stories in the Bible, I thought about my friend, Reverend Leon Burrows, the ecumenical minister at Smith College. I asked the student if he would like to write to somebody who has read all the stories in the Bible to see if he would come and talk with us about this question (see Figure 3.1). Being a public school teacher wary of the separation of church and state, I decided to mention this to my principal, who is very supportive but likes to know what's going on. I told her that my student was writing to invite Rev. Burroughs to visit and discuss this question. And while there might be hesitations about God entering the public school classroom, this inquiry was not about teaching religion. My principal agreed that it was an interesting question and suggested that my students also write to invite a parent in the school, Rabbi David, who could offer another perspective.

In the letters of invitation to Rabbi David and Reverend Burrows (see Figure 3.1), the students filled them in about our philosophical discussion regarding bravery. The children decided that if the rabbi and the minister were going to take time to come and talk with them about their important question, they should give the visitors a gift. Students decided that they would compile a book of their ideas about bravery. They wrote philosophical essays on the nature of bravery—and used examples from stories read in class. Students used many examples from the biographies of activists we'd read together in class: Gandhi, Sojourner Truth, Harriet Tubman, as well as family members. When the minister and the rabbi came for their interview, the students gave each of them a copy of this collection of essays on bravery. Both clergy used the book the children collectively authored in their sermons that very weekend—sharing the children's perspectives with their congregations.

The main and central question the children asked the rabbi and the minister was "Was there a time when God was ever scared?" The children were surprised that Rabbi David did not answer their question, but began to ask them more questions. Reverend Burrows joined the conversation and brought a New Testament perspective, telling the story of when Jesus was facing crucifixion. The children and I had a rich and fascinating discussion with both clergy. While no other class I taught before or since ever raised the question, "Was God ever scared?" these 20 children really cared about this question—thus it was important and critical for them.

## The Teacher's Perspective

When I reflect on the practice of using interviews, I think about the potential of adding multiple voices, perspectives, and points of view to my class. While many people have the impulse to "Google" everything, there is great value in listening to the stories of families and community members—which are so much richer, relatable, and present a variety of perspectives. Through interviews, I want children to see themselves

Figure 3.1. Invitation to a Philosophical Discussion on the Nature of Bravery

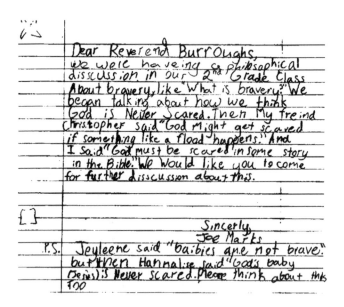

Dear Reverend Burroughs,

We were haveing a philosophical disscussion in our 2nd Grade Class About bravery, like "What is bravery?" We began talking about how we think God is Never Scared. Then My freind Christopher said "God might get scared if something like a flood happens." And I said "God must be scared in some story in the Bible." We Would like you to come for further disscussion about this.

                                                    Sincerly,
                                                    Joe Marks

P.S. Jeyleene said "baibies are not brave." but then Hannalise said "God's baby (Jesus) is Never scared. Please think about this Too as knowledgeable and capable—as opposed to relying on an Internet search engine in order to answer questions. I steer that impulse in a different direction—in response to "let's Google it," I say, "Who could we ask?" and use that as an opportunity to build relationships. My students learn that they can get so much more from an interview and from a relationship than they could from reading an impersonal answer on a computer screen.

Students often rally behind a question that they find compelling—maybe a question that one student raises stimulates another student to add more—and then it has a snowball effect. They all work with the question and develop a sense of community ownership. When students find a compelling question, they will own it completely. They will keep asking it and asking it. Parents have often told me over the years how their children have asked their friends, relatives, and neighbors these questions, in their quest to find answers.

For teachers who may have more regimented classrooms, think about how interviews relate to multiple areas of the curriculum—and simultaneously address multiple curricular objectives. Pursuing big questions through interviews does not mean taking time away from learning, but represents curriculum integration in meaningful, relevant, situated, and multicultural ways. For example, in exploring "Was there ever a time when God was scared?" my students delved into the English Language Arts curriculum framework—reading, writing, listening, and speaking. This came to life through the read aloud, the initial discussion, the crafting of questions, the letters of invitation, and the collection of essays which referred back to previous texts and discussions.

Whenever I have a philosophical discussion in my class, I transcribe (or ask my student teacher to) as I facilitate the discussion. It is important to write down on chart paper everything that the students are saying, exactly as they are saying it (verbatim), and not try to correct their grammar or standardize their English. By doing so, students come to respect differences and see each other as worthy and capable human beings. It is also important to write their names by what they said so they feel a sense of ownership. I want the group to value their ideas, not quibble over their grammar. This allows students to point to the chart as they agree and extend, or when they disagree and pose a counterexample and say: "When Joe said . . . ". Or "When Jeyleene said that Jesus was a baby and was afraid to get a shot . . . " they can point to the chart and build their arguments accordingly. By doing that, they are developing strong oral language skills, the ability to make a persuasive argument and use evidence—from the text, from the discussion, etc. Then students can transfer these habits to writing persuasive essays because they have learned to refer to the text as they consider a classmate's opinion, going back to quote what someone previously said, weighing evidence, as they develop their own argument.

Through these authentic oral language experiences students develop listening and speaking skills, with high motivation to comprehend others' ideas and clearly articulate their own. Interviews, as well as philosophical discussions, are excellent pre-writing activities in preparing to write interview questions or letters of invitation or thanks, or to write a summary of what they learned from the interview. They are reading throughout the process: referring back to the text of the story, the text of the discussion, reading their interview questions, reading the notes on the chart documenting what the interviewee(s) said. While the interview with the two clergy primarily focused on standards for English Language Arts, it also tied in with Social Studies through the picture book biographies we read about Sojourner Truth, Gandhi, Harriet Tubman, and other historic leaders. While these examples are biographies, they also relate to history because they are not isolated life stories; they're within historical and social contexts of slavery and colonialism. These biographies came to life in the children's philosophical essays on the nature of bravery. Interviews can and do address multiple standards, within and across curricular areas, meaningfully becoming a site not only for multicultural education but for curriculum integration.

People often ask me, "How can you get away with teaching like this?" In answering, I draw on my experience as a community organizer. I was often asked to arrange funerals for people: farmworkers without families, homeless people who had frozen to death, people who had been involved in the community for years. Over the years, I attended many funerals, mostly Christian, and noticed that many different clergy often used the same (or at least similar) readings. Yet, interestingly, different clergy offered different interpretations of the very same Bible stories, putting their own spin on the same text. That's "biblical interpretation." That's what I do with the state standards and the Common Core State Standards (CCSS). First, you must know the standards well—so that if someone is even tempted to get in your face with, "Why are you teaching 2nd-graders about Gandhi?" or "Sojourner Truth isn't on the curriculum for 2nd-graders," then you are able to say "Well, Sojourner Truth per se is not part of our Social Studies curriculum, but we do study biography as part of our ELA (English Language Arts) standards." You have to be able to justify, in light of your interpretation of the standards, why you are doing what you are doing—why you are teaching what you are teaching.

The ELA framework is a rationale for exploring many different things related to an interview approach to multicultural teaching and learning. If children have these kinds of prior experiences, when they write their long composition essay in 4th grade on the state standardized test, they know how to participate in a philosophical discussion, how to agree and extend by using an example from real life, another example from the text. Or students can convincingly disagree and pose a counterexample, going back to what someone said that they disagree with, and they can give a counterexample from their life, from history, from the text. It is important to know the standards for your grade level, but also for what is coming ahead, not because you want to push down standards, but because you want to make visible the powerful learning that is happening in your classroom in ways that are going to add validity to what you are doing.

## REFLECTING ON INTERVIEWS AS A
## STRATEGY FOR TEACHING MULTICULTURALLY

Through asking questions, we can expand the traditional curriculum, what is currently present and sanctioned in schools. It is important to engage in listening to the voices, questions, and concerns of the children but also bring in the voices and stories of school and community members, of those who are traditionally outsiders, to each interview. Asking questions, bringing in voices that are and have been historically absent are advantages of interviews as an approach to multicultural teaching and learning.

Interviews address a variety of content areas and standards. In addition to the ELA framework Ms. Cowhey discussed earlier, social studies (the social, cultural, and historical context of the interviews) and mathematics (data collection, processing, and representation) are also relevant areas often addressed via interviews. And mathematics tends to be an unsung hero in multicultural education, yet the data unit and standards related to it are really aligned with interview-based teaching.

For new teachers who are getting started with interviews as a way to teach more equitably, one of the most important practices is to really listen. Listen, listen, listen! As teachers, we may feel that there is an external pressure, or internalized pressure, to talk, talk, talk. While we are leaders in the classroom, we may put too much pressure on ourselves to keep talking, to be the only one talking. We know that it is very hard to talk and listen at the same time. This is especially the case when you don't want students to talk while you are talking. So—the first thing is to be purposeful and deliberate in sharing the talking space in the classroom. And if children know that you truly listen and their questions are valued, then you get into a positive loop, in which more questions are asked; they ask bigger questions, better questions. Students will know that their questions matter and will lead to an authentic and meaningful learning journey. Shine spotlights onto questions that students ask. If you cannot address the question at that very moment, write it down so that you can get back to the exact question—as voiced by the student—at another time. Listening to and valuing questions is an important starting place.

Listening is then balanced by a really thorough knowledge of the standards, framework, or curriculum adopted by your (pre)school. Then you can clearly link children's questions and interviews to what is supposed to be happening—because it is! As you read and learn the about the mandated standards, framework, and curriculum, you will need to develop a very thorough knowledge of the parts of that framework that are most open to interpretation. So, really know your data strand for the math standards if you are teaching 2nd grade in Massachusetts—or whatever strands and standards are most open to interpretation in your own setting—whether you are teaching preschoolers or 2nd-graders, in California, Texas, or elsewhere.

Develop relationships with families and community members, so that when something comes up, when a big question is asked, you know who to go to—or have a network of people who will help you identify possible experts to be interviewed. Build and keep relationships across time and space—authentically. Assume that people will say yes to your interview invitation. Ask people to come in—you'll find they respect teachers who are trying to make their teaching more authentic and they respect children who have questions to ask. Forge relationships but don't hesitate to reach beyond these relationships to expand the teaching and learning that go on in your classroom. Ask questions as you seek to identify experts. Value questions, listen, and make room for talk in your own classroom.

Finally, encourage students to ask questions. Don't stop them from "interrupting" and asking questions, but invite them to ask questions—cultivate their sense of curiosity and inquiry. Even if their questions are representations of conflict, embrace them. Conflict represents a wonderful opportunity for learning—and interviews can provide spaces for multiple and even conflicting perspectives, experiences, points of view, and knowledge to be considered. Why not give it a try? After all, interviews are inexpensive, relevant, responsive, and malleable (in terms of time and space). Interviews can make teaching and learning more meaningful in your classroom.

## FURTHER RESOURCES

Cowhey, M. (2006). *Black ants and Buddhists: Thinking critically and teaching differently in the primary grades.* Portland, MN: Stenhouse.

Rogovin, P. (1998). *Classroom interviews: A world of learning.* Portsmouth, NH: Heinemann.

# CHAPTER 4

# Critical Inquiry:
# Supporting Children's Investigations

Learning is experiencing the world (Dewey, 1938). In experiencing the world, children put forth hypotheses and test them. For example, as kindergartners go from the classroom to the playground after a rainy morning, they may find mud puddles. They may wonder: What if I jump in the mud puddle? Will my shoes get wet? Will my socks get wet? Will my feet get wet? Why? Then, they may jump right in to find out—to test their hypothesis. After jumping in and realizing that their socks did or did not get wet and that their feet did or did not get wet, they hurry to tell their friends and their teacher(s) about their findings. They disseminate their findings after testing their hypothesis. Young children inquire much of the time—they act in ways that test space, time, and material boundaries. Inquiry is a way of life for young children. So, why not bring this way of life to the forefront of the teaching and learning that takes place in early childhood classrooms?

Adults have traditionally viewed inquiry as more formal research—the scientific method and procedures, involving stating a hypothesis along with data collection and analysis (Jennings & Mills, 2009). Here, from a critical multicultural perspective and in the early childhood classroom, inquiry involves teachers and students who engage in "grand conversations" (Wells, 1995) and in both "wondering" and "information-seeking" forms of dialogue (Lindfors, 1999). This concept is further explained below.

## WHY CRITICAL INQUIRY AS A STRATEGY
## FOR TEACHING MULTICULTURALLY?

Inquiry does not have a formula. It cannot. It emerges out of the questions and interests of students who are members of a classroom community of learners. And since each community is different, each inquiry journey will be unique. From a critical perspective, inquiry is multicultural because it transforms the curriculum in ways that address both personal and culturally relevant teaching as well as rigorous educational opportunities. It departs from the notion of curriculum as static and separate from the lives of young children. Young children's questions are at the core of an inquiry-based curriculum.

From the students' interests, inquiry expands and grows to address and approach a variety of content areas. Inquiry brings together content areas in interdisciplinary and authentic ways through students' questions and interests. It brings together a variety of backgrounds and resources—some of which are typically included in the traditional classroom, and others that are not. Inquiry is a space where the personal and academic converge and craft an interdisciplinary and culturally relevant curriculum (Cowhey, 2006; Mills & Donnelly, 2001; Mills, O'Keefe, & Whitin, 1996).

Inquiry is multicultural because it uses multiple perspectives while engaging learners in a knowledge-construction process. From an inquiry perspective, learners collectively uncover the social and cultural influences of knowledge and its creation. As learners ask questions, they consider the multiple ways to pursue answers, thus considering many perspectives that are socially and culturally located (Banks, 2007). Inquiry has the potential to foster the development of positive attitudes and actions toward diverse groups. Finally, inquiry can come to life as equity pedagogy, which encompasses culturally relevant practices, thus restructuring the classroom environment.

## WAYS TO ENGAGE IN
## CRITICAL INQUIRY

Critical inquiries are interdisciplinary learning opportunities regarding issues that are critical for the children who are part of a classroom learning community. They differ from themes and units as the teacher listens to the children and seizes opportunities for pursuing questions. In critical inquiry, questions matter. An important part of inquiry in the early childhood classroom is dialogue (Freire, 1970; Lindfors, 1999; Wells, 1999)—consideration of a variety of perspectives and learning from and with others. It is respecting and revering differences as providing additional and valuable insights. Teachers and learners co-construct knowledge as they talk, learn, and delve deeper into their inquiry.

An important part of inquiry is the sense of historicity of the learning journey, awareness of decisions made and of resources employed. When she was a junior kindergarten teacher in Canada, Vivian Vasquez (2004) used audit trails to chronologically document the inquiry journeys of the 3- to 5-year-old children she taught, making a visual display—an audit trail— of their learning journey. This aided the community of learners to sustain a topic of inquiry over a long period of time. Together, Vasquez and the young children who made up her classroom community engaged in inquiry about beluga whales, reading from a variety of sources and inquiring into fiction and nonfiction accounts. They also inquired into McDonald's Happy Meals—why they were made and marketed, and how they targeted children when not even their Happy Meal toys came in child-safe bags. (For more about these inquiries, see Vasquez, 2004.)

Seeking to honor the history and the context of the inquiries that went on in her classroom, Mary Cowhey (the teacher featured in Chapter 3) created newsletters that not only documented the inquiry undertaken by the children in her classroom, but also reached a wider audience. These student-authored newsletters involved families in learnings by telling stories of inquiries-in-progress taking place in her 1st- and 2nd-grade classrooms and served to expand their inquiry. The 6- to 8-year-old children in Ms. Cowhey's classroom also wrote about their inquiry for a local education publication.

## GETTING STARTED

To get started, a teacher must listen to the children and place the children's interests and questions at the center of the curriculum—not being oppressed or bullied by standards or guides. This does not mean that standards will go unmet—it means that they will be addressed in a context that is authentic and interesting to the classroom community. In listening to children and the questions they have, teachers can seize important moments and topics, bringing together children's interests and academic demands in seamless and meaningful ways.

It may be fruitful not to deflect questions or interjections that may initially seem to be disruptive, but to explore those topics and questions that draw energy and interest from the group. As a topic is determined and starts being pursued, it is important to document its history in the context of the classroom—the history of the community's journey with that topic. There are many ways of documenting this journey such as audit trails (Vasquez, 2004), book writing, and newsletters. Such documentation also serves to plan for an integrated curriculum, offering the teacher and students opportunities to return to a previously explored aspect of the topic of inquiry. It is important to acknowledge that when getting started, it is difficult to know how long the inquiry will last—so any topic may become an extended topic of inquiry. In Mary Cowhey's forthcoming narrative, 2nd-grade students moved from exclaiming in the middle of a read aloud that their teddy bears were naked to exploring how clothing is made and where children's clothing came from. So to start, just listen, jump in, and document your journey, knowing that you won't have all the answers or resources—and that this is the way inquiry begins.

## CONSIDERING OBSTACLES, EXPLORING POSSIBILITIES

Inquiry takes time—it is not a tool, but a strategy, an approach that shapes a classroom's teaching and learning (Mills, O'Keefe, & Jennings, 2004). As such, it respects the individuality and diversities of learning experiences, backgrounds, and abilities in a classroom—it does not impose time constraints or one-size-fits-all standardized ways of teaching. It honors the breathtaking diversities of schoolchildren (Genishi & Dyson, 2009).

From a critical perspective, the possibilities afforded by inquiry include expanding the teaching and learning that goes on in your classroom in significant and meaningful ways. From a critical perspective, inquiry is not simply following the scientific method, not simply testing hypotheses. It is more about understanding the world in which we live. It is about inviting students to engage in research to answer questions that truly matters to them. In other words, for teachers, inquiry is about creating the space for children to see themselves as capable and worthy human beings, inviting them to be researchers and to systematically learn from a variety of sources representing multiple perspectives and points of view. It is about going beyond what is to be taught, thinking of standards as the floor rather than as the ceiling. And while a variety of tools (such as interviews and multicultural books) can be part of inquiry, inquiry cannot be a tool that is part of another approach to teaching. Inquiry is a strategy, an approach to teaching.

Through inquiry, teachers use children's interests to craft an interdisciplinary curriculum that is at once critical, multicultural, and rigorous (addressing standards and curricular goals). This is a wonderful opportunity but can also be a challenge since it requires that the teacher know the standards and curriculum for his or her grade level (and beyond) very well. So, the work of the teacher in regard to standards is to look at what is happening and identify which standards are being addressed within the authentic learning that is going on. In doing so, the teacher can extend and expand learning opportunities to address even more standards. Nevertheless, addressing the standards does not mean standardizing teaching and learning.

One way to bring inquiry to life in an early childhood classroom is to listen more and talk less. Too much teacher talk is an obstacle to learning through inquiry. The teacher must identify and use students' energy and excitement for learning about their topic of interest as he or she engages them in a learning journey that can encompass multiple areas of the curriculum. For example, social studies (economics, geography, history), mathematics, language arts, and science are applied when inquiring how clothing is made. This is all done while placing issues of equity front and center. So, the children's interests and questions become a locomotive to which other areas of the curriculum can be connected in meaningful and exciting ways. It takes time, but it is worth the effort.

Aside from time and space, the biggest obstacle to reimagining the demands associated with the standardization of education is the courage to admit that you don't know it all—and that you will be learning from and with your students. It is the act of embracing a humble stance that blurs the roles of teacher and learner. In doing so, you help students understand that the books present in your classroom portray incomplete accounts and that there are human resources beyond the classroom walls that can further the learning journey of that specific community. In doing so, you will help your students see that their learning community extends beyond the classroom walls. In considering and addressing this obstacle, remember that you don't have to have perfect answers to questions and comprehensive things to say all the time—even if (after the fact) you think of what you should or could have said. Welcome the opportunity to learn with the children who are members of your classroom communities and make room for multiple voices, perspectives, and points of view to be considered.

## ENACTING CRITICAL INQUIRY IN AN EARLY CHILDHOOD SETTING

What does an early childhood classroom look like when a teacher uses critical inquiry to support children's investigations and teach multiculturally? There is no formula for the perfect classroom inquiry since the topics of study, the group of children and families, as well as the resources available will be particular to specific times and spaces. Thus while there are many ways to bring critical inquiry to life in early childhood classrooms, here I invite you to listen closely to Mary Cowhey (whom you met in Chapter 3) and learn how critical inquiry came to life in her 2nd-grade class.

### The Teacher

As no one tool or strategy works for everyone, some teachers choose to use a variety of approaches for teaching equitably. Mary Cowhey is one of those teachers. Her mission as a teacher is to teach children within the context of their community. She sees communities, families, students, and teachers learning together, thus forging possibilities for positive change. She emphasizes that we all bring biases to what we do—whether or not we admit it—and her bias is to look closely at the experience of low-income students, being very critical of school as an institution.

Mary points out that biases are inherent to America's schooling institutions—a system that discriminates against low-income people, single parents, English language learners, and many others. She believes that even though she works in a wonderful school with excellent leadership, she must be vigilant and aware of that because schools as institutions are structured to privilege White, middle-class, educated, English-speaking, professional families. She constantly tries to look at school through the eyes of her students who are struggling the most, who are the most marginalized. In doing so, she considers how she can contribute to making schools more empowering rather than disempowering. In the next two sections, Mary writes in her own voice about engaging in critical inquiry in her 2nd-grade classroom.

## *The Classroom*

How we can make the experience of education transformative? That is, not something students have to endure, survive, put up with, or slog through—but something that they can really embrace, that they feel they could use, that could transform their lives, that could be their ticket to what they want. School needs to be a nurturing place, where they can figure out what they want. Initiating and pursuing inquiry projects centered on student-generated questions can be an important part of figuring out what they want to learn and do in their lives.

One year we distributed teddy bears in my 2nd-grade classroom to support children's emotional health (see *Bears, Bears Everywhere!* by Lesley Koplow, 2008). One day after recess, as my students settled onto the rug with their teddy bears for our read aloud, one child gasped, "My teddy bear is naked!" The panic spread like wildfire as all the students realized their teddy bears were naked. My students had completely lost interest in the book I wanted to read aloud. I sighed, said the teddy bears looked fine to me, but asked if they wanted to do something about this situation. They said that in 1st grade they had made clothes for their bears.

Not being a craft-inclined teacher, I asked how they made clothes for their bears. They said that Evan's dad came in with a sewing machine to help them sew the clothes. After much talk, they decided to make vests for their new bears, and invited Evan's dad, Peter, to come in with his sewing machine. I figured this would be a good way to counter gender stereotypes. I remembered from a home visit that another student's mother was a quilter. I asked for her help. She made a simple vest pattern for us and donated a bag of ribbons. I dug out a box of felt rectangles and a coffee can of buttons we use when learning about attributes in math. Evan's dad came with his sewing machine. Each child traced the pattern on a piece of felt, learned to sew a vest with ribbon trim and a button, and selected a ribbon for the bear's necktie.

My students were very excited about their dressed teddy bears, so I decided to channel that enthusiasm into a writing activity. They each drew a detailed portrait of their previously identical teddy bears. Then, they wrote a detailed description of their teddy bear, detailing the attributes of its necktie and vest with the button and ribbon trim. We hung up all the teddy portraits in the hallway, like a little rogue's gallery. Then we mixed up the written descriptions and hung them underneath. My students (and most of the other 1st- and 2nd-graders in the school) read the descriptions and carefully figured out which teddy bear portrait matched. Since we were studying attributes in math, we decided to use the dressed teddy bears to play our "Guess My Rule" attribute game. Right about then I was starting to feel pretty done with the teddy bears and their vests.

But no, it was not to be. One of my students, Brandon, brought in an old book from the 1960s called *How We Get Our Clothing* (McCall, 1961). He had gone home very excited about making the vests, told his family about it, and had been busy sewing at home. His mother found this old book for him. The book was full of stereotypes, referring to the workers as workmen, even though many were female seamstresses. I set the book aside, thinking that I would read it myself at lunchtime and then use it for a critical reading activity in the afternoon. Brandon, however, was very interested in the book and brought it when we went to the library. He begged me to read it right then. Someone once told me that a teacher should never read aloud a book to the class that she hasn't read herself beforehand. Cornered by Brandon, I broke that rule. I pointed out the copyright date, 1961. The children were fascinated by the black and white photos, the details of clothing manufacturing. On page 13, I showed them a photo of White women with beehive hairdos and cat eye glasses working at sewing machines and dutifully read the caption, which said, "Much of our clothing is made in factories like this one." I looked at the children and said, "Actually, that's a lie." They gasped. I went on, "Well, it used to be true, when this book was written. This is where my clothing was made when I was your age. Lots of adults in my neighborhood in Brooklyn worked in clothing factories, and they were all members of the International Ladies Garment Workers Union, which meant a better life for them and their kids. In the 1970s there was a TV commercial for the ILGWU with a song that began: 'Look for the union label / When you are buying a coat, dress, or blouse.'"

To my amazement, I remembered the whole song, and when I finished singing, Brandon asked, "Where should we look for it?" "Look for what?" I responded. "The union label, you said we should look for it." I chuckled, "Oh, they meant the label in the back of your shirt, but you won't find. . . ." The children weren't listening to me. Quick as a wink, they were slipping their arms out of their sleeves and turning their shirts backwards to look at their labels, or pushing away their friends' ponytails and tugging at their shirt tags, trying to pronounce Malaysia and Lesotho. They wanted to know why their labels didn't say "Made in the USA" as in the end of the song. I explained that nowadays, most of our clothes are made outside the United States. Lots of questions bubbled up. "Why don't they make clothes in the United States anymore? Who makes our clothes now? Does it matter where clothes are made?" The children kept looking at tags (see Figure 4.1). My students began to make connections between where their clothes were made and the countries their classmates were from. "Gonzalo, my t-shirt was made in Mexico, where you're from!" or "Vien, my sneakers are made in Vietnam. That's your country!"

We lined up to head back to class for a snack, stopping at the bathroom to wash up. Usually I have to hassle the students to all get in there and wash their hands, but on this particular day, they all went in without a single reminder. I stood alone in the hallway, thinking that I hadn't planned on them freaking out about naked teddy bears or teaching them how to sew tiny vests. I was able to harness that enthusiasm and use it to meet objectives in English Language Arts and in our mathematical study of attributes. Now I hadn't planned on this sudden obsession with where our shirts were made, and I tried to think of a way we could use it.

My approach is to listen to and watch children, to be ready to catch these eruptions of curiosity. I also need to know my standards and curriculum frameworks well enough so that I can think creatively about how to connect that curiosity with a learning objective. When kids come up with an authentic question that they're ready to pursue with passion and energy, I can use that question and driving curiosity like a locomotive to power their learning. I can start by hooking one curricular objective to it. If that locomotive's energy keeps building, I can hook on more

**Figure 4.1. Reading Shirt Labels**

Source: Cowhey, 2009, p. 15

objectives, like more freight cars. The way I can "fit it" into my schedule is by thoroughly integrating it into our day, across our morning meeting, math, social studies, reading and writing, and read aloud.

We were still in our data unit in math, having finished up with attributes; we were moving on to gathering and representing data. Instead of gathering data about how many teeth students in other classes and grades had lost, as we usually do in our math curriculum, I thought we could use shirt label data instead. I also considered how our 2nd-grade standards include a unit on maps and globes, with children beginning to learn the continents and some countries on each continent. I was planning to do that later in the year, but I could move it up. Then I noticed I was still alone in the hallway and hustled the kids out of the bathroom. As they lined up in the hallway, I noticed they were whispering to each other. I moved closer to listen and heard a child whisper, "My pants were made in Egypt."

Back in the classroom, as the children took out their snacks, I put globes or world maps on each table and pulled down the world map in the front of the classroom. I started by asking them to find the continents on the map, which I listed on the easel. Then I asked them to work in their groups to find the country where their shirt was made and figure out what continent it was on. They got busy, scouring their maps and globes, often going over to classmates for help, "You're from Cambodia, right? Can you show me where Cambodia is?" Then we went around the room, with each child saying where his or her shirt was from and (with the help of the table group) which continent it was on, as I put a tally mark next to that continent. I asked them what they noticed from our graph and what they wondered. Again, lots more questions came up, like why there were so many marks for Asia, why most of the marks for North America were for countries in Central America and the Caribbean, and were there really factories in Africa?

That night I looked up the union song on YouTube and learned that there had been a whole series of union commercials, which are still studied in business schools today as a brilliant (though sadly unsuccessful) piece of commercial marketing. The commercials were unique in those days in that they used real union members, not professional singers or actresses. I remembered that the workers were of all races, short and tall, fat and thin, wearing glasses and regular street clothes. I wrote down the lyrics to show my students at morning meeting.

The next day, when I told my students what I'd learned, they wanted to learn to sing the union song themselves in spite of some difficult vocabulary for English language learners, like "blouse" and "wages." When I showed them a video of the original ILGWU commercial, they wanted to know when they could make a commercial like that.

Challenged by technology, I sought help from a former student who was then in high school, and his favorite classes were video production and Latin. He was happy to help my students videotape a commercial and borrowed the necessary equipment from his video teacher. The children staged their commercial to look like the original, with one child singing at first, and more and more children joining with each line, carrying props to illustrate the lyrics. The high school student did a very professional job editing the video and earned extra credit in his video class.

One homework assignment during this inquiry was for the children to learn how their family sorted the laundry. While every family has laundry (a commonality), each family has a particular way of sorting laundry (a potential difference). The first part of the assignment was to learn the family's criteria for sorting laundry. Then they were to sort the laundry for their family, take one basket of laundry they had sorted, and look at all the labels to learn where the clothing was made. They brought that data to class. Together, the children had a ton of data—data that they could relate to, not some numbers in a book as part of a worksheet. There was a lot of discussion about how they would represent the data. They settled on a color scheme for continents and cut small label-sized rectangles of different colors. If they had a shirt made in Mexico, they wrote "Mexico" on a red rectangle and pasted it beside North America on their graph. They made 6-foot-long graphs representing the data they'd collected (see Figure 4.2). As they organized countries within continents, they kept referring back to their maps and globes and learned a lot of geography.

The graphs and the visual representation of data generated many questions. I wanted my students to do more than just gather and represent data. I wanted them to analyze it. I invited the children to think about "What do you notice when you look at these graphs? What do you wonder?" They noted that there were very few labels from Australia and none from Antarctica, which led to an interesting discussion of the presence of international science stations there but the absence of people native to Antarctica. But mostly they noted that their clothing largely came from Asia, Africa, and Central America. The children asked questions such as: "How come there are so few labels from North America?" and "Why do most of the labels from North America really come from Central America or the Caribbean, not USA?" Most of the "made in the USA" labels were from older clothing like some of my own clothing purchased at thrift stores in town. They also realized that "made in the USA" labels were much easier to find at thrift stores than at Walmart, Old Navy, or Target. The children deliberately looked for "made in the USA" labels in those stores and couldn't find any. The children came to the conclusion (and action) that as shoppers they had the right to ask to see the manager of the store where they shop and to say: "I am a Walmart

Figure 4.2. Graphing Labels

Source: Cowhey, 2009, p. 16

shopper. I would like to buy clothes that say 'made in the USA.' I would like to see more clothes with a 'made in the USA' label here at Walmart." And while they recognized that this action may not immediately change Walmart and its purchasing practices, they also came to the conclusion that there was no reason not to exert that pressure on Walmart, to exert power as a consumer. The children realized that they could push back and think critically—not only in my classroom, but also beyond the walls of the classroom and the school. They realized that they could (and should) think and look before they buy.

During our inquiry the children had a lot of questions about unions, what they were, why people made them, and if we couldn't find any ILGWU labels, then where did the union go? This was a perfect fit for our economics objectives: learning about goods and services, consumers and producers. To introduce students to ideas of collective action, organizing, solidarity, striking and negotiating, I read aloud picture books like *Swimmy* (Lioni, 1963), *Farmer Duck* (Waddell & Oxenbury, 1991), and *Click, Clack, Moo: Cows That Type* (Cronin, 2000). I also read books like

*Harvesting Hope: The Story of Cesar Chavez* (Krull, 2003), about Cesar Chavez and the United Farm Workers, and *¡Sí, Se Puede! / Yes, We Can!: Janitor Strike In L.A.* (Cohn, 2002) about Service Employees International Union and their Justice for Janitors Campaign. We learned about the sanitation workers' strike that brought Martin Luther King Jr. to Memphis, where he was assassinated.

At the same time we were engaged in this inquiry, we learned that workers at the local Stop and Shop (a unionized grocery store in town) were threatening to strike. When students went grocery shopping with their parents, they read the workers' buttons and asked them questions. Nearly daily, children asked questions or shared updates about the supermarket workers, their demands of health benefits for part-time workers, and brought in news articles about the local negotiations and labor news in other places. The children learned more new vocabulary, like health benefits and contracts. My students kept vocabulary notebooks, where they collected new words they wanted to learn. One of the students noticed he had a lot of new words related to our inquiry. He proposed we make a "Protesters' Dictionary."

For the Protesters' Dictionary, the children made their own definitions of these words—e.g., *strike, boycott, union, organize, solidarity.* They decided what was going to be included and why. Some words came from our inquiry and from books we'd read. Other words came from newspaper articles and family conversations. Words from these various sources became the basis for the dictionary—bringing together community words, adult words (from newspaper stories), along with words from children's picture books. They co-constructed a powerful representation of a complex concept and captured the collective power of a union—that workers gain power by being part of a union.

In their "Protesters' Dictionary," under *negotiate,* they had drawn a person with a talking bubble that said, "We want money for helf. we need it." The children had a depth of understanding of the issues, but at the same time, they were 7- and 8-year-olds who did not yet spell conventionally—yet this did not hinder their understanding of these important civic issues.

Of course, I wondered how much of all this the children grasped. One day a boy arrived late, during morning meeting, when we were discussing the supermarket workers. A student on the rug said, "Hey, Joe, the Stop and Shop workers settled!" Joe asked, "So what did they get?" His informant responded: "They got the health benefits for all the workers." "All right!" Joe cheered, pumping his fist in the air. These 2nd-graders knew the importance of getting health benefits for all workers—regardless of whether they worked part time or full time. And they knew about the power of collectively protesting, of striking, of demanding better working conditions.

To share our learning, we invited families to the classroom. The children told the story of their inquiry, how they pursued their question. All of our guests checked their shirt labels and entered the data on a new graph, adding their observations and questions to our analysis. They looked at all the graphs the children made and asked them questions. We presented our Protesters' Dictionary and showed our Look for the Union Label commercial.

## The Teacher's Perspective

This inquiry learning ran for about 2 months. It started with the exclamation about the naked teddy bears, which I thought I'd settled by following the suggestion that we sew vests for the bears. At first, I'd connected that interest with the work on attributes we were doing in the beginning of our data unit in mathematics and used the dressed bears as a subject for nonfiction descriptive writing and reading in language arts. Brandon's obsession with how clothing was made led to his bringing in the old book, which sparked my memory of the Look for The Union Label song, which in turn kicked off shirt-label reading. That happened to coincide with our data unit work on gathering, representing, and analyzing data. I was able to move forward with my whole social studies unit about geography and our study of continents and cultures, to integrate that with our data work on the labels. Even as we were finishing the data unit and our huge graphs of label data, interest and energy was still growing, fueled in part by the impending supermarket strike. Again, using children's curiosity as the locomotive that was driving this inquiry, I was able to hook on another standards freight car, our economics objectives, exploring the roles of consumers and producers.

While our 2nd-grade social studies unit doesn't include labor history, our language arts curriculum includes biographies of leaders, so we read biographies of labor leaders. We read about Cesar Chavez and other activists and their relation to labor, like Martin Luther King Jr. and the Memphis sanitation workers' strike. We also read about Gandhi, our hero who made his khadi himself from thread he spun and cloth he wove from Indian cotton, rather than wearing clothing made in Britain, the colonial ruler of India. Our read alouds throughout this period tied in to our inquiry and built vocabulary, as did our morning meeting discussion of labor-related news articles and current events. Back to English Language Arts, we built academic vocabulary with our Protesters' Dictionary. We were even able to address standards in media and technology (standards I'm normally not too strong on) through studying the ILGWU commercial campaign and recording our own commercial of the song. We never investigated where our shirts were from instead of our 2nd-grade curriculum. In fact, we used the inquiry to ignite our 2nd-grade curriculum, to teach it all in a deeper and more connected way than I could have without the motivation of the inquiry project. I did not envision this full-blown, complicated, integrated curricular map as I stood alone in the hallway outside the bathroom while my students checked the labels to see where their pants were made. It grew organically, fueled by lively student, family, and community dialogue, spreading like the vigorous roots of raspberry plants, popping up in other curricular areas, bearing fruit all over the place.

If you think that that you couldn't teach this way because you don't have the content knowledge to support children's wide-ranging inquiry, remember that you just have to be ready to learn and to practice learning anything from everyone. Don't limit yourself to teaching your students what you already know. Name what you want to learn. Model being a lifelong learner. Enjoy yourself as you learn with your students.

## REFLECTING ON CRITICAL INQUIRY AS A STRATEGY FOR TEACHING MULTICULTURALLY

In teaching multiculturally, it is essential to start with what matters to children. The question of where clothing was made mattered to the children in Ms. Cowhey's class. And in pursuing this question, lots of interesting socioeconomic issues came up. Over time, the children realized that the older clothing had a higher percentage of "made in the USA" labels than newer clothing, which is largely made in other countries. As a class, they talked about the meaning of such time and space connections to clothing and workers' rights.

By peeking into Mary Cowhey's classroom, we can see that inquiry is a powerful strategy for teaching multiculturally. Why not give it a try in your own classroom? After all, inquiry is interdisciplinary, relevant, and responsive to children's interests and questions as well as a powerful way to bring mandated standards to life in authentic and integrated ways. Inquiry can make teaching and learning more meaningful in your classroom.

## FURTHER RESOURCES

Cowhey, M. (2006). *Black ants and Buddhists: Thinking critically and teaching differently in the primary grades.* Portland, MN: Stenhouse.

Cowhey, M. (2009). "Where's your shirt from?" Second graders learn to use data to change the world. *Connect, 23*(2), 14–17. http://www.mcowhey.com/

Koplow, L. (2008). *Bears, bears everywhere! Supporting children's emotional health in the classroom*. New York: Teachers College Press.

Long, S. (2011). *Supporting students in a time of core standards: English language arts grades prek–2*. Urbana, IL: National Council of Teachers of English.

Mills, H., & Donnelly, A. (Eds). (2001). *From the ground up: Creating a culture of inquiry*. Portsmouth: Heinemann.

Mills, H., O'Keefe, T., & Jennings, L. (2004). *Looking closely and listening carefully: Learning literacy through inquiry*. Urbana, IL: National Council of Teachers of English.

Vasquez, V. (2004). *Negotiating critical literacies with young children*. Mahwah, NJ: Lawrence Erlbaum Associates.

*Note:* If you want to learn more about the wonderful teacher featured in Chapter 3 and Chapter 4, please visit Mary Cowhey's website: http://www.mcowhey.com.

# CHAPTER 5

# Culture Circles with Multicultural Literature: Addressing Issues of Fairness

This is not fair! How can we change it? Young children are committed to issues of fairness (Paley, 1986). So, when young children come to see a situation as unfair, they often call it out. As teachers, we may hear, "Briana is not letting me play. It's not fair," or "Why do we have to clean up? Not fair!" Sometimes these issues of fairness are more in-the-moment frustrations. Other times, they affect many broader interactions in the classroom. So, instead of brushing off those "not fair" comments, it is important to pay close attention to the issues that young children identify as unfair. Nevertheless, issues of (un)fairness are so commonplace that they may not be challenged—by children or by teacher(s). They are just dismissed as "the way things are." "Why?" and "How can we change it?" are important and powerful questions as we seek to name and change unfair practices and inequitable issues in our own classrooms and (pre)schools.

Upon identifying and considering the unfair issue, children may want to move beyond what *is* happening to *why* it is happening, by dialoguing and negotiating spaces for change—addressing the "How can we change it?" question. And *it* can mean anything that is part of their lives. So, fill in the blank—whatever the important *it* may be for the children you teach (or hope to teach). Remember that critical issues must be critical to students—and not be imposed by the teacher(s). The issue at hand has to be real and relevant to matter to the children. After all, every day young children invite us adults to make the invisible and familiar, visible. Every day they question and change practices that promote unfairness and inequity in our own classrooms and (pre)schools.

Culture circles are fertile grounds for addressing such issues of fairness. In culture circles, children can name and question inequities, moving toward changing the world in which they live. "A culture circle is a group of individuals involved in learning . . . the political analysis of their immediate reality. . . . In culture circles, reading demands more than decodification of linguistic symbols. It is viewed as political 'reading' of the world" (Giroux, 1985, p. viii). While this approach may appear to be beyond the scope of an early childhood classroom, it is indeed relatable to the children as it takes on issues of (un)fairness that emanate from their very lives. Teachers can seize unfair practices and situations as opportunities for learning through the use of problem posing to initiate dialogue in their classroms through culture circles. In establishing a culture circle, the first task of the critical educator is to deconstruct authoritarian modes of discourse in conventional class-rooms (Shor, 1990). Sitting in circles is a great way to disrupt authoritarian teacher-student relationships.

## WHY CULTURE CIRCLES AS A WAY OF TEACHING MULTICULTURALLY?

Culture circles employ a generative approach to education (which starts from the concerns, experiences, and knowledge of its participants, children and adults). In culture circles, students are/become participants, and their experiences are valued as central to the construction of meaning. A culture circle starts from participants' individual and collective experiences, from what matters to the children who are members of the classroom community. The teacher begins by thematically investigating the realities and practices of children in his or her classroom, and then codifying those realities into multicultural children's books, which serve as grounds for the classroom community to engage in questioning and problematization (Souto-Manning, 2010b). Through asking questions about what is (the status quo), children begin dialogue and collectively negotiate spaces for change, for en-visioning what could be. Culture circles are multicultural as they consider a variety of perspectives and honor participants' background experiences and knowledge as worthy. Culture circles can occur during typical circle or meeting time, common in many early childhood classes, or at other times during the day.

Culture circles are grounded in the belief that "no educational experi-ence takes place in a vacuum, only in a real context—historical, economic, political, and not necessarily identical to any other context" (Freire, 1985, p. 12). In culture circles, teachers facilitate the process of questioning what is (the status quo), while valuing and building upon previous experiences of the individuals within each community of learners. Collectively, mem-bers of culture circles consider conditions that shaped shared situations of unfairness. Since worlds and words are socially and historically located, to be able to challenge and change their worlds, individuals need to name the issues of unfairness and inequity affecting them—by asking questions such as "How did this happen?" and "What caused this?" Such questions can get at the real issues, assessing larger structures that influence individual lives as well as larger ideas and concepts that infiltrate everyday talk. In this way, individuals not only problematize their locations, but also move away from those locations by looking into the forces and structures that have histori-cally framed instances of unfairness.

Multicultural education focuses on reforming curriculum content and classroom teaching, and culture circles do just that—they move away from a model in which the teacher is the sole expert, where curriculum is predetermined, and where information is accepted at face value (Giroux, 1992). Culture circles foster a space in which teacher and learner roles are blurred, in which the teacher becomes a facilitator who creates a space for questions to be asked as opposed to being the one having the answers to every question. Culture circles fashion curriculum from students' lives and experiences and create a way of teaching in which multiple perspectives and points of view are considered. From the perspective of culture circles, education includes considering and problematizing specific situations within particular contexts. To do so, it questions issues of power in society.

## WAYS TO USE CULTURE CIRCLES WITH MULTICULTURAL LITERATURE

Culture circles can come to life in a variety of settings—yet they cannot be directly imported—they must be re-created so that they honor the context of each community and its individual members (Freire, 1998). While culture circles are conceptualized as a strategy, multicultural books can be tools within culture circles, used as situated representations of issues of inequity affecting classroom actions and interactions. There is no predetermined formula for the implementation of culture circles. Yet, its common aspects are generative themes, problem posing, dialogue, and problem-solving leading to action. These five dynamic phases may be described as follows:

1. *Generative themes.* During this phase, situated representations of common happenings are identified via thematic investigations of the children's interests, lives, and practices. A prominent and recurring happening (a phenomenon) is then codified and represented by a multicultural children's book which is read.
2. *Problem posing.* During this phase, the representational artifact read—the multicultural children's book representing a particular situation—is decoded through children's questions. These questions seek to uncover the reasons shaping such happenings or situations. The focus is on reading between the lines as well as recognizing social, cultural, and historical forces shaping the specific issue.
3. *Dialogue.* This happens throughout the culture circle, as participating children consider multiple perspectives and move from posing problems to collectively negotiating solutions. This is not a distinct phase as it starts with the problems and questions being posed and moves into problem-solving and action. Here, listening

and thinking about a multitude of perspectives is essential so that participants can uncover and recognize the ways in which varying points of view impact how children are positioned.

4. *Problem-solving.* This is the phase in which participating children offer ways to change the issue being considered in their own settings, in situated ways. Contextual specifics are taken into account as well as personal preferences. The idea is not to arrive at one simple solution, but to think about a variety of possibilities that are real and may come to life. Possible solutions will be as unique as the members of the group who are part of the culture circle. The key is to make visible the influences shaping children's inequitable actions, situations, and beliefs, and examine them, question them, collectively move toward co-constructing possible solutions, and envisioning possibilities.

5. *Action* (at the personal and/or societal level). Solutions negotiated through dialogue are context-specific, implemented at the personal and/or societal level, and may lead to heightened awareness of the importance of not making assumptions—of not imposing one's understandings onto others and of always questioning one's own beliefs and practices instead of justifying such beliefs and practices with "this is just the way it is" rationalizations.

The phases of culture circles come to life differently and are constantly being renegotiated—because children's voices and ideas, what matters to them, are at the center. Culture circles do not focus on the transmission or mastery of some specific body of knowledge. As participants approach a situation, they consider multiple perspectives and problematize the issues in a critically conscious way. Thus, through dialogue, individuals can reframe education as a problem posing process, problematizing what is as opposed to seeking quick fixes and clear-cut solutions.

## GETTING STARTED

Culture circles can be seen as a vehicle for bringing together multiple areas of the curriculum—a space for meaningful, interdisciplinary, multicultural teaching and learning. As for getting culture circles started, I suggest paying close attention to what children say, observing their actions and interactions while seeking to find common issues of inequity. Then, find a book that represents a shared issue of inequity affecting the lives of several children. This can be done at circle time, meeting time, morning message, or read aloud time. These are natural times and spaces in many early childhood classrooms to get started with culture circles.

To implement culture circles, it is essential to get to know the tools—multicultural children's books—and have them ready in your classroom regardless of your class membership. This may sound simple, but it isn't. Although it was 50 years ago that *The Snowy Day* (Keats, 1962) was published as the first children's book featuring an African American main character (Bishop, 2007), there is still a prevalence of books in print that feature White characters from heterosexual families who speak Mainstream American English. In addition, Newbery Award and Honor books from 1975 to 2009 feature a disproportionately smaller percentage of children with disabilities and ethnic diversity than actual classroom demographics throughout the United States (Israelsen-Hartley, 2010). Nonetheless, now there are publishing houses that favor culturally relevant books, such as Cinco Puntos Press, Lee and Low, Tricycle Press, Children's Book Press, and Piñata Books. Figure 5.1 provides a sampling of multicultural books organized by focus, although many of them address more than one focus.

Having a variety of multicultural children's books available is essential. As a teacher, it is important to consider who wrote the book and ask yourself questions such as the following:

- What are the potential strengths of this book? What is silenced or ignored by this book? (All diversity books, activities, or artifacts do not have to be inclusive of all areas of diversity; focus on what is not said or suggested about the specific diversity on which the material is focused.)
- How can this book be used to support the children whose culture is most greatly reflected in it? How can the children who may not understand or relate to the culture most greatly reflected in it use this book?

And be sure that there are books that portray multiple diversities—such as race, socioeconomics, gender, sexuality, and ability—in your classroom. Whether or not your classroom community reflects these diversities, it is important that the classroom materials be inclusive. We are educating children for a multicultural society, so our classroom materials should reflect this goal.

## CONSIDERING OBSTACLES, EXPLORING POSSIBILITIES

Culture circles are grounded in problem posing, critical dialogue, and problem-solving, thus fostering higher order thinking skills and clearly fostering problem-solving skills—two goals of any evidence-based educational agenda. Yet, culture circles do so equitably. The aim of culture circles is

Figure 5.1. Preschool–2nd-Grade Multicultural Literature Sampler

**Gender and Sexuality**

*And Tango Makes Three* (by Richardson & Parnell)
*Antonio's Card/La Tarjeta de Antonio* (by González)
*My Princess Boy* (by Kilodavis)
*Nasreen's Secret School: A True Story from Afghanistan* (by Winter)

**Race and Racism**

*Ellington Was Not a Street* (by Shange & Nelson)
*Freedom Summer* (by Wiles)
*Goin' Someplace Special* (by McKissack)
*Henry's Freedom Box* (by Levine)
*My People* (by Hughes)
*Please, Baby, Please* (by Lee & Lewis Lee)
*White Socks Only* (by Coleman)

**Spirituality**

*He's Got The Whole World in His Hands* (by Nelson)
*Let It Shine: Three Favorite Spirituals* (by Bryan)
*The Three Questions* (by Muth)
*What a Wonderful World* (by Weiss and Thiel)
*Willoughby and the Lion* (by Foley)
*Zen Shorts* (by Muth)

**Homelessness and Low-Income Families**

*A Shelter in Our Car* (by Gunning)
*Beatrice's Goat* (by McBrier)
*Fly Away Home* (by Bunting)
*Gettin' Through Thursday* (by Cooper)
*One Hen: How One Small Loan Made a Big Difference* (by Milway)
*Something Beautiful* (by Wyeth)
*Those Shoes* (by Boelts)
*Uncle Willie and the Soup Kitchen* (by DiSalvo-Ryan)

**Considering Multiple Perspectives**

*Good Luck Bear* (by Foley)
*Multiple versions of: Three Little Pigs, Little Red Riding Hood*
*Purple Little Bird* (by Foley)
*Voices in the Park* (by Browne)
*We're Different, We're the Same, and We're All Wonderful!* (by Kates)

**Immigration**

*I Love Saturdays y Domingos* (by Ada)
*My Diary from Here to There/Mi Diario de Aqui Hasta Alla* (by Perez)
*Super Cilantro Girl* (by Herrera)

*(continued)*

**Figure 5.1.** *(continued)*

### Immigrants and School Entry

*I Am René, the Boy/Soy René El Niño* (by Colato Laínez)
*La Mariposa* (by Jiménez)
*My Name is Yoon* (by Recorvits)
*One Green Apple* (by Bunting)
*René Has Two Last Names/René Tiene Dos Apellidos* (by Colato Laínez)
*The Name Jar* (by Choi)
*The Upside Down Boy/El Niño De Cabeza* (by Herrera)

### Culturally Specific Practices and Celebrations in the United States

*Book Fiesta!: Celebrate Children's Day/Book Day/
    Celebremos el día de los niños/El día de los libros* (by Mora)
*Just in Case: A Trickster Tale and Spanish Alphabet Book* (by Yuyi Morales)
*Just a Minute: A Trickster Tale and Counting Book* (by Yuyi Morales)
*Lion Dancer: Ernie Wan's Chinese New Year* (by Waters & Slovenz-Low)
*New Year at the Pier: A Rosh Hashanah Story* (by Wayland)
*Too Many Tamales* (by Gary Soto)

### Japanese American Internment

*Baseball Saved Us* (by Mochizuki)
*Home of the Brave* (by Say)
*The Bracelet* (by Uchida)

### Native Stories

*Jingle Dancer* (by Smith)
*Shi-shi-etko* (by Campbell)
*Thanks to the Animals* (by Sockabasin)

### Multiple Languages and Ways of Communicating

*A Day's Work* (by Bunting)
*Hooway for Wodney Wat* (by Lester)
*I Ain't Gonna Paint No More* (by Beaumont)
*Tickle Tickle* (by Hru)

### Dis/Abilities

*Apt. 3* (by Keats)
*Hi, I'm Ben! . . . and I've Got a Secret!* (by Bouwkamp)
*My Brother Charlie* (by Peete)
*Rolling Along: The Story of Taylor and His Wheelchair* (by Heelan)

### Growing Up in The City

*C is for City* (by Grimes)
*Five Little Gefiltes* (by Horowitz)
*Tar Beach* (by Ringgold)
*Uptown* (by Collier)
*What Can You Do with a Paleta?/¿Qué Puedes Hacer con una Paleta?* (by Tafolla)

*Note:* For full publication information, see "Children's Books" at the back of this book.

"conscientization," or critical meta-awareness, of each participant's condition (Freire, 1970). They create spaces for students to be positioned as agents of change who collectively engage in the social analysis of the issues affecting their own actions and interactions inequitably. Thus, the possibilities are many—and so are the topics to be explored.

One of the challenges of engaging in culture circles is that the teacher does not know exactly where the dialogue is headed, consistent with the very premise of critical pedagogy. Circles are "space[s] in which all views can be voiced freely and safely. Only when all views are heard can we claim that the heterogeneous nature of our culture is most widely represented in the circle" (Steiner, Krank, McLaren, & Bahruth, 2000, p. 123). It can be hard to step out of the way, to listen instead of talking, to facilitate—but it is a necessary practice if we are to truly honor diversities in culture circles.

Preschool teacher Dana Frantz Bentley (or Dana as her preschoolers call her) emphasizes that one of the main obstacles to doing this kind of work is recognizing one's own self as a cultural being. For her, it was hard to accept that she occupies many categories of privilege—being White, college educated, heterosexual, and a speaker of Mainstream American English. As she engaged in transforming herself and recognizing her multiple positions of privilege, she explored racism (looking into the realities and implications of racial identities), experienced disequilibrium (feeling sad, angry, and overwhelmed), reached out (becoming part of a group of multicultural early childhood educators), and is now engaging in critical multicultural teaching (Derman-Sparks & Ramsey, 2011). She believes that one must constantly examine his or her own privileges and problematize his or her actions, points of view, and positionings based on these privileges. Thus one of the challenges of this work is that you as a teacher must come to understand your own self as a cultural being and be meta-aware of the privileges afforded to you by specific facets of your identity (as outlined in Chapter 2).

Finding a place for this kind of democratic teaching in your classroom can be a challenge—especially within the context of traditional (pre)schools. While culture circles can easily fit within a project approach or inquiry-based curriculum, they do not fit easily within the context of over-regimented curriculum goals and guides. Thus, it is important to highlight the way that conventional skills and practices are learned in unconventional yet meaningful ways within culture circles. Making this learning visible to families and administrators is key. Dana suggests that this can be made easier by forging strong relationships with families—then children and their families become advocates.

Keeping family members informed of classroom happenings is important—as is allowing them to ask questions and come in at any time. While some teachers may fear parents' and families' resistance to culture circles, Dana found that when the children were excited about learning (in culture circles) and their parents were informed (via a daily email chronicling the children's pursuits), there were no surprises and great support:

I try to set up a dynamic where I am in constant communication with the parents. If they have a problem, they know that I am the first person they should come to. And that's hard, because it means that they have my cell phone number and that I am checking email and emailing back and forth with them late into the night sometimes. But it is also about showing them that I genuinely care for their children. So, if one of them is having a good day at school, I just shoot [the family] an email and tell them. . . .We are constantly engaging in these conversations so that they know that we are on a team for their child, that we are a unit for and with their child. . . . Once they know the level of my care for their child, I've found that they are more comfortable letting me take chances.

Dana invites families to see how the children themselves bring up the themes being problematized. Making that visible is essential for families to understand that someone's viewpoint is not being imposed on their children, but they are becoming problem posers and problem-solvers in their own right. This is important because family members also have prejudices and naturally bring their assumptions and beliefs into the mix. "But once you show them that you care for their child and that you are not imposing your views, but honoring the children's questions and interests, then it shifts the balance of everything," says Dana.

## ENACTING CULTURE CIRCLES WITH MULTICULTURAL LITERATURE IN AN EARLY CHILDHOOD SETTING

What does an early childhood classroom look like when a teacher uses culture circles with multicultural literature to address issues of fairness and teach multiculturally? While there are many ways to bring culture circles to life in early childhood classrooms, here I invite you to enter Dana Frantz Bentley's preschool classroom and learn how culture circles came to life in her preschool classroom. Let's begin by learning about the teacher and the school where she teaches.

### The Teacher

Dana Frantz Bentley is a preschool teacher at Buckingham Browne & Nichols School, an independent school in Cambridge, Massachusetts. The school has around 1,000 students from birth through 12th grade. The demographics of the student population are 74% White and 26% students of color. Although 27% of its students attend on a full financial aid package, others pay between $20,000 and $30,000 annually in tuition. Dana has been an early childhood teacher for 10 years—in three distinct settings. She started teaching right after receiving her undergraduate degree—she got a fellowship to teach in an outreach program in Boston public housing.

When she started teaching, as the only White teacher in the school and the only teacher who had a college education, she was met with a less than familiar environment. Most of the children in the school were African American, so for the first time in her life, Dana felt like an outsider. Nevertheless, she was determined to learn from and with the children and their families as well as from the teachers in the school. And she did—she acknowledges that her African American co-teacher was key to her growth as a teacher of African American children. While teaching in Boston, Dana got a master's degree from Harvard. Then, she moved to New York City and got a doctorate from Teachers College, Columbia University. During this time in New York City, she taught at the Rita Gold Early Childhood Center at Teachers College.

After her doctorate, Dana decided to follow her passion to teach young children. Multicultural practices are, according to Dana, the most important part of how she conducts herself in the classroom, how she plans, how she succeeds—and fails—in working with her students. She states: "In order to authentically engage in multicultural teaching, you have to be willing to fail. You have to be willing to ask yourself every day: 'What did I help enable and what did I disable? How can I do better in helping to enable?'" Dana believes that critical multicultural teaching in the early years involves problematizing one's own practices, acknowledging the failures, and transforming what is into what could be, always seeking to foster better educational experiences for young children.

Dana sees her mission as a teacher to create spaces for the voices of children to be heard. She sees young children as uniquely capable and powerful. She does not believe in saving or rescuing children, but in creating spaces for their unique and powerful voices to be heard and to shape the teaching and learning that happen in the classroom. She sees her role as not only promoting these voices, but also in challenging and problematizing what is said by children, so that they come to more nuanced understandings of the world in which they live. She has high expectations for the children she teaches, encouraging them to own their voices and opinions while problematizing their understandings, moving toward respecting and valuing diversities.

## The Classroom

During the first week of the school year, upon welcoming her 4-year-old preschoolers, Dana asked them to challenge their beliefs. Dana invited the children to sit down in a circle and asked them: "Who is in charge?" Hands flew into the air, all wanting to get the "right" answer. Their common and repeated response was "The teacher." They proceeded to dialogue for about 30 minutes, and instead of providing them with an answer, Dana kept asking questions. She asked: "Who's going be doing the work?" and "Who is going be doing the playing?" and finally "Who do you really think should be in charge?" and "Who's going to have the ideas?" Right then, they started a very important conversation. Dana began her year with a culture circle—by reading children's assumptions as a text, problematizing them, talking about them, and moving toward a reconceptualization of classroom power and dynamics. There was a shift—the children moved from believing that the teachers were in charge to understanding that they were in charge—after all, they would be the ones generating the ideas, playing, and working. They came to see themselves as making many decisions in the classroom, being in charge of the curriculum, and being responsible for their community. Later in the year, one of the children explained: "We are in charge and a lot of times we have different ideas and we have to listen to other people's ideas. If somebody doesn't agree, you have to negotiate and then you have to talk about it. It's not fair if even one person doesn't agree." Dana saw this shift as a necessary starting point for the work she does in her preschool classroom.

In Dana's classroom, culture circles take place at meeting time. Dana calls this time "meetings," to signify a space where serious work is done and where hard issues are undertaken. It is extremely important to first establish a community where children respect each other and where there is trust. A circle needs to be envisioned as a democratic and participatory learning space—where children and teachers can talk about issues that are uncomfortable for them. In Dana's classroom, meeting time is perceived as a participatory space where all voices are heard and valued. Culture circles are a central component of her classroom practice. She has always thought of the circle as a place for coming together as a community—a place where the members of the classroom community can see each other and hear each other in a more equitable way:

It is about the physicality of it, a space where we hear voices, where we respond to each other in thoughtful and respectful ways. It's also a space for each child's voice to be heard on the same level as the teachers' voices. In a circle, no one is at the front, no one is at the back, no one is standing, so it is a more equitable space. We are all sitting; we all occupy a similar space. It is a space to connect as a community.

Dana sits cross-legged in the circle with the children and raises her hand when she wants to contribute, waiting for the children who are assuming leadership roles to call on her—indicating a respect for the children and challenging the hierarchy of teachers' voices being more valuable than children's voices.

In Dana's preschool classroom, the community engages in at least two circles per day—one in the beginning of the formalized day (after 1 full hour of free play) and one at the end. Sometimes the children request one or two meetings in between, as they understand the classroom circle as a space where ideas can be generated, discussed, and problematized. Culture circles are a platform for them as individuals and also for them as a community.

In the beginning of the year, she invites children to take charge of the meetings and to ask questions. There is no hard-set agenda at first—except for doing away with the typical hierarchy, power structures, and roles typically present in classrooms. They learn to balance the power and to be more inclusive and respectful of all members of the classroom community. Yet, Dana acknowledges that no matter how child-centered a teacher wants or claims to be, as a critical educator you must acknowledge that you come in with an agenda—and that your identity as a teacher affords you certain powers and privileges. The important thing is to be flexible and responsive—letting go of a planned agenda if the children take the dialogue and ensuing pedagogical decisions in a new direction. While Dana has ideas and plans for the day, she acknowledges that her ideas are not nearly as important as theirs. Thus circles are spaces where her ideas may get pushed aside and where ideas put forth by the children get highlighted. Then, she has to pick up and go in the direction the community decides. After all, the children decide what is critical.

## "What's Her Name?" A Story of Gender-Color Stereotypes

One day, one of the girls in Dana's preschool class, Ashlee, was sharing a story about her purple pony. Upon concluding, Ashlee said: "I'm ready for questions." Immediately, Andrew raised his hand and asked: "What's her name?" And before Ashlee could answer, John asked: "Why does it have to be a her?" Looking confused, Andrew said: "Because she is purple." At the time, John who had a purple cast on his hand said: "My favorite color is purple." This led to a grand conversation. Anthony, Dana's co-teacher (who was facilitating the activity at the time), started gesturing to Dana so that she could join the conversation (she had been cleaning paint and observing what was going on from a distance, but not leading the activity).

As Dana walked over, she invited the children to start considering the questions at hand: "Do certain colors belong to certain kids? Do certain colors belong to girls and some to boys?" The children began talking and thinking about it. They were really trying to figure this out. Then Thomas asked: "Can girls only play princess and boys can only play *Star Wars*? Is that fair?" Dana asked: "Is it fair to only allow certain kids to play with certain things or to choose certain colors because they are boys or because they are girls?" This conversation occurred within a context in which the children were used to considering issues of justice, fairness, and equality and had participated in this kind of dialogic learning many times before (Bentley, 2011).

As Dana was talking with the children, facilitating the discussion that identified the issue, her co-teacher Anthony grabbed *My Princess Boy* (Kilodavis, 2010) for her to read to the children. *My Princess Boy* is a book about Dyson, a boy who loves the color pink and sparkly things. Sometimes he wears dresses and sometimes jeans. He likes to wear his princess tiara and to climb trees. He's a Princess Boy and his family loves him just the way he is. *My Princess Boy* codified the generative theme which had emerged in the classroom.

Dana introduced the book with a personal story. She told the children about Kye, a boy in a former class who loved to dress up in princess dresses, "I loved Kye. He was a great kid, and he loved to wear princess dresses and princess heels. I told him that it was okay. What do you guys think about that?" The children in Dana's class responded: "Oh, that's okay" and "He liked to play, so that's okay" and "You're the teacher and you said it was okay, so it's okay." Then, she told them how the other teachers at the school thought that was bad. She explained how they came into her classroom and advised her to make Kye stop wearing those dresses, that it wasn't okay, and the boy shouldn't be allowed to do that. And then she asked them: "So—what do you think about that?" And they thought about it—remaining silent for what seemed like a long time—then started saying things such as: "That's mean" and "I think that made him feel really bad." The children wanted to know what she did about it—and she said that she told him that wearing a dress was fine and that people should wear whatever made them feel good and happy.

As Dana was reading *My Princess Boy* slowly, allowing time for the children to ask questions, Camille, one of the girls said: "That's just really weird." And Dana, who confesses that every muscle in her body was tense, tried not to blurt out, "That's not okay. It's not okay to talk like this." Dana took a deep breath and asked Camille, "Why do you think it's weird? Can you tell us more about what you are thinking?" As Dana kept listening, Camille explained what she was thinking, that boys usually don't wear dresses. Then one of the other children said: "But that's not fair. Do you think it is fair to say that because a boy wears a dress he is weird?" This launched a whole other discussion as the children considered whether it was weird for boys to wear dresses or for girls to dress as knights or to wear pants (which many of them were wearing). The children were fascinated with knights at that point, and one of the little girls, Marisa, who loved to dress in knight costumes, said: "Well, I love being a knight. Why can't a boy be a princess?" Marisa's observations evolved into a very engaged dialogue, during which the children were not solely trying to defend their views, but to understand other points of view and perspectives present in the classroom. As a class, they stopped what they were doing to pursue this issue—which had become urgent and critical in the context of their classroom.

Dana read *My Princess Boy* every day that week. She wanted the children to really be able to talk it out and to challenge their assumptions about gender and dress as well as gender and color associations. The children asked Dana to tell the story of Kye—her personal experience with gender-based stereotypes and inequities—each time prior to reading the book *My Princess Boy*. That made the story very relatable and real for the children—after all, this was not just a story from a book, but Dana's story of another preschooler. The talk shifted from deeming Princess Boy to be weird to a dialogue seeking to understand how Kye felt. At first, the children came to dub the teachers who had told Dana she should not let Kye wear princess dresses "the mean teachers." Then, as time passed, they came to understand how the teachers' behaviors were similar to what had happened in the classroom when Andrew assumed that purple was a girl color. They started considering: How did John feel when another child immediately assumed that purple was for girls? And where is this belief coming from? They started talking about colors of clothes, toys, and ads. They started realizing that it was not what they really believed in—just what they had been told over and over, thus coming to believe it.

In their classroom, they started questioning their assumptions about clothing and colors being associated with specific genders. Some of them (including Dana) had blue eyes—a color typically associated with boys. What would she do if as a girl she weren't allowed to wear blue? And who decided that blue is for boys and pink and purple for girls? Do we believe in it? These were some of the questions considered along with questions about fairness and rights (Bentley, 2011). Here are some others: Is it fair that we think that's weird? When we say that, what does it mean for the boy who likes to be a princess? The idea of fairness and particularly the idea of fairness during play was key to children as they defined what counted as critical for them. The children centered their questions on these issues. When we play, can girls be knights? Is it fair to say, "Hey, only boys can be knights!"? Is it fair to say that a boy cannot like pink? Or purple?

Dana recounts that in her classroom the culture circle about gender stereotypes took place across a couple of weeks, including several daily meetings to talk about issues of gender stereotypes. Now, every time someone says something that employs gender stereotypical ideas and discourses in the classroom, a child will say "Remember Kye?" or "Remember *My Princess Boy*?" and that invites them to problematize what they are doing in the moment. These personal reference points invite responses such as: "It's okay if you want to wear a crown" and "It's okay if you want to be Luke Skywalker. Girls can be Luke Skywalker." But they do it for themselves. Dana is not the one saying these things and inviting them to problematize their actions. It is an authentic process where they go up to each other and say, "If you want to be Princess Leia, you can be Princess Leia, John. That's fine, boys can do that even if some grown-ups don't think so."

## The Teacher's Perspective

The children in Dana's class moved toward problem-solving and action (in terms of their beliefs and practices) at the end of the first dialogue, but because this was such a big issue and they were still thinking about it, Dana saw a need to re-establish that culture circle multiple times. This allowed time and space to acknowledge children's discomfort and move toward a place where they were identifying what their real beliefs were and what they had come to believe just because they'd heard something so many times—that blue is for boys and pink (and purple) is for girls. She needed to acknowledge and respect the children's own time instead of imposing hers. According to Dana,

> The teacher needs to recognize the point where, as a community, there is peace. Initially, there is a huge wave and the ocean gets very troubled and you are trying to work through these things together. At times, there are clashes—and the children know that this is just our working through these troubled waters. But there comes a point where all of the ripples are dying down and they've worked through it, and they are comfortable with it and they know every word of the book that was read. They are still asking those questions—of themselves or others—because they are aware of the issue, but they are answering them for themselves. That's the point where I feel that we are peaceful again and we are ready to move on to something else, the point where they take ownership of the issue.

Dana acknowledges that as teachers we may try to deal with these very important issues too quickly and say, "I had the bodies conversation," "I had the gender conversation," or "We've done that," but then it's all about what you as a teacher did. However, each class, each group of children has to work through the unique questions that arise. As a teacher, instead of hurrying, you may have to wait until you get to the point in which the children you teach have carefully and thoroughly problematized an issue, engaged in meaningful dialogue, learned from each other and considered a variety of perspectives. Then coming to problem-solve together, the community decides on an action that can be emotional (changing the emotions associated with the issue or how the issue is seen) or instrumental (taking action).

The important thing, Dana reminds us, is how the children are making sense of these issues, how they are problematizing their own actions and beliefs that were initially taken for granted. Instead of taking their rote answers (as children often repeat what their teachers or parents have said), it is important to invite young children to make sense of their own beliefs and of their worlds. As a community, the children in Dana's preschool classroom invited each other to become more inclusive and equitable while problematizing and refuting discourses and associations promoted by society at large. The children started realizing how gender had affected their experiences in a variety of settings. So, while there was no big "take to the streets" action, the children enacted change in their own behaviors, words, actions, and interactions.

Dana says that it is important for social justice (issues of fairness and equity) to be part of the teaching and learning in the early childhood classroom, but that many times teachers' understandings of social justice are not relatable to the children they teach. It is very hard for teachers to pluck these larger issues out of the sky and put them down for the children to mess around with, to problematize, to challenge their understandings, and to truly consider more socially just actions and structures in their classrooms. But it is necessary. Thus, Dana creates a space where she harvests opportunities generated from children's actions and interactions, out of the children's questions, conflicts, and discomforts.

Having someone to live these practices with you can be a truly empowering experience. Dana shares:

> My co-teacher Anthony is the person who makes these practices possible. His presence, the questions that he poses and the role that he plays in responding to my questions are essential to diversity practices in our classroom. There is something about having that critical perspective right there with me every day. . . . My co-teacher is the person who recognizes when I am teaching at my best, and also the one who I trust to challenge me when I am falling short. This is particularly important when considering the practice of multiculturalism in the classroom. That voice of support from someone who knows you best is a solace and foundation through the inherent uncertainties which are a part of multicultural practices. That same relationship provides a safe space for challenges and questioning. This whole process is really about trust. Because of the trust and faith that I have in Anthony and in our co-teaching relationship, new questions and challenges in our multicultural practice become possible. I am not afraid to be wrong or to take a leap of faith, because we do so as a unit. Each leap we take is the function of our discourse, our challenges and support of one another. I don't know what these practices would look like without my teaching partner. This relationship makes so many things possible.

# REFLECTING ON CULTURE CIRCLES AS A WAY
# OF TEACHING MULTICULTURALLY

As you read earlier, when a child attributed a gender to a pony based on the color of the pony, Dana explored a variety of teaching and learning possibilities through looking at issues of gender stereotypes, moving beyond the color issue to clothing and roles in play as well. She admits that it is important to get comfortable with this approach of seizing opportunities to address issues of fairness in the classroom even when other things have been planned. It is also important to accept the fact that in culture circles, children will engage in conversations that may make the teacher really uncomfortable. Yet, it is a worthy journey when students are calling out and naming unfair and inequitable assumptions. In Dana's preschool classroom, they were making issues visible while challenging normative gender definitions, structures, and ways of playing.

Tackling social justice issues that are relevant to children's lives is thus key. And to learn about these issues, it is important to:

- Make time for children to engage in play and authentic interaction;
- Listen closely to what children say and the stories they construct;
- Carefully consider their questions—even when you feel like shutting them down because they sound inappropriate;
- Bring those questions and issues to the center of your teaching;
- Create real connections with the children you teach—if you are asking them to take risks, do the same and share your stories and experiences;
- Create a classroom environment where problem posing is valued— enabling children to delve deeper by asking questions, but never giving ready, canned answers to their questions or fixed solutions to their problems and issues.

Listen carefully and be willing to step into the discomfort. Always be ready with questions—because culture circles are about problematizing what is. It would have been easier for Dana to say to Camille: "That's not fair. We can like any color we want" and move on. Instead, she decided to lift that moment, making it a wonderful learning opportunity. Had she given an answer such as that, she would have shut down a huge learning opportunity—to address issues of social justice which are relevant and relatable to her students. Thus, questions are more important than answers. Let children's questions grow instead of shutting them down, extending what the children say with prompts such as "Why do you think that? I think that's really interesting." As teachers we always step on some conversations that should be allowed to grow—that is going to happen. But instead of focusing on lamenting missed opportunities, it is important to focus on the next conversation that can become the center of a culture circle.

In her classroom, when Dana asks "What do you think?" she does not have a correct response in mind. She asks the question to better understand the child and his/her meaning-making process. She also asks, "What do you know?" "How do you know that?" "What makes you think this way?" In doing so, she encourages the children she teaches to name and problematize what makes them uncomfortable. But this understanding does not appear without any effort. We teachers have to teach students to ask questions, to name issues, and then really prove to them that their questions matter by placing those questions front and center in the classroom.

And remember, culture circles have to develop within the context of the communities where they take place. So, create an atmosphere in which students are comfortable disagreeing and where disagreements and tensions can become wonderful learning opportunities, acknowledging that often as a teacher your main mission should not be to soothe and resolve, but to incite dialogue about inequitable issues—to invite children to step into the discomfort with you. Recognize that supporting children as learners may mean agitating them at times. Sometimes helping them grow means pushing them harder and making them uncomfortable so that they can come to a place of even greater comfort at the end—after they have worked through discomfort. Let your students learn from and with each other as they explore critical issues. In Dana's experience, the community is always stronger in the end—and more respectful and appreciative of diversities as strengths.

## FURTHER RESOURCES

Bentley, D. F. (in press). *Everyday artists: Inquiry and creativity in the early childhood classroom.* New York: Teachers College Press.

Freire, P. (1973). *Education for critical consciousness.* New York: Seabury Press.

Freire, P., & Macedo, D. (1987). *Literacy: Reading the word and the world.* Westport, CT: Bergin & Garvey.

Souto-Manning, M. (2010b). *Freire, teaching, and learning: Culture circles across contexts.* New York: Peter Lang.

# CHAPTER 6

# Community Resources and Home Literacies: Developing Funds of Knowledge

"Do you like the dollar store?" "Where you get yo hairdid?" "You goin' to church Tuesday?" "How 'bout 'Pretty Boy Swag'?" As children get to know and interact with each other, they talk about the places where they live, the spaces they inhabit, and the communities of which they are a part. They talk about the practices taking place in their homes and communities—listening to Soulja Boy's "Pretty Boy Swag," getting hairdid, and going to church. Communities and homes are inherent parts of the lives of young children. As teachers who seek to build on the strengths of the children we teach, instead of judging children's homes and community practices against our own preconceived notions of "appropriate" and "best," we can make community resources and home literacy practices (home literacies) central to our teaching and visible in our classrooms. After all, if we are to build on what children already know, why wouldn't we want to build on children's home literacies and community resources in our own classrooms?

"Where are you from?" is thus an important question to consider when teaching young children in multicultural and equitable ways. And I do not mean only countries, states, and cities where children were born—but the communities and homes where they live, the important people in their lives. So, in this chapter, we explore ways in which community resources and home literacies can lead to more equitable, multicultural, and culturally relevant teaching and learning spaces in the early childhood classroom. Further, we explore authentic ways to access these community resources and home literacies and employ them in the classroom to the advantage of our students. By doing so, we create educational spaces that are at once rigorous and value the places and practices that are important to the children we teach.

## WHY COMMUNITY RESOURCES AND HOME LITERACIES AS TOOLS FOR TEACHING MULTICULTURALLY?

Home literacy practices and community resources have deep and lasting influences on learning. As we teachers try to understand and find ways to better teach all children in our classrooms and (pre)schools, we must consider that community resources and home literacies have positive influences on academic success and "can significantly contribute to the developing picture of complex and synergistic relationships among home literacy practice and linguistic capital within contexts of power, language, hegemony, and textual resources" (Purcell-Gates, 2007, p. 212).

A comprehensive view of home literacies and community resources recognizes that young children's languages, literacies, and learning processes are not linear or static. As teachers, we need to pay close attention to individual children, learning from and with them, their families, and communities (Gregory, Long, & Volk, 2004). It is important to acknowledge that young children are active members of different groups and learn how to function within each of them. When teachers value and build on students' practices in home and community contexts and bring such practices to the classroom, they can foster more responsive and equitable learning experiences.

Young children live in a variety of contexts—homes, schools, and communities, for example—and each of these contexts functions according to specific rules and customs. As young children are developing school language and literacy practices and experiencing different linguistic and cultural systems at home (Heath, 1983), they develop ways of participating in each one of these contexts. Thus, it is important for the teacher to know that these rules of participation vary across specific contexts (such as home and school) and can be mediated in ways that build on the strengths of the child's home and community practices—on what is already familiar to them. Instead of remaining silent and making young children feel that they do not belong or are not competent in school, teachers can cast a positive light onto these often marginalized home languages (such as African American Language and Spanish) and literacies (such as singing hymns, displaying call-and-response discourse patterns, and engaging in oral storytelling).

Teachers can foster more culturally relevant classrooms by creating spaces in the curriculum where there is a merging of personal and curricular spaces. The merging of these two spaces allows students to draw on specific ways of knowing within and across contexts. When this merging does not come to life naturally, it must be negotiated by the teacher who genuinely positions herself or himself as a learner of the children's home and community practices—realizing that there are no cookie-cutter, one-size-fits-all approaches and that each child will be unique even if from the same community and racial background as others. Then, these practices can be brought to the classroom, being refined and redesigned in collaboration between teacher and students (Souto-Manning, 2010a). For this to take place, teachers' and students' community resources and home literacies must be identified and examined.

Community resources and home literacies have been called "funds of knowledge" that can "transform classrooms into more advanced contexts for teaching and learning" (Moll & Greenberg, 1990, p. 344). In coming to recognize the value and power of these funds of knowledge, we teachers can come to see families as resources who "contribute substantively to the development of our lessons . . . [and] to the content and process of classroom learning" (p. 339). This approach to teaching requires a broader interpretation of what counts as literacy; to include the practices families and communities engage in—those practices that inform children's cultural and linguistic worlds. This view opens up the doors to valuing what each child already knows instead of conceptualizing certain children as if they need to be fixed.

While home and school literacy tools may be apparently similar, when the rules of participation change starkly between home and school, the tools no longer seem useful or relevant (Lewis, Enciso, & Moje, 2007). If at home children are socialized into literacy practices that have rules of participation closely aligned with school practices and discourses, they are more likely to be successful in school. If such rules of participation differ, children are likely to experience disequilibrium and develop a poor sense of self in school. Teachers are more likely to employ rules of participation which are coherent with their own primary literacy models, aligned with their own home practices and schooling experiences (Haddix, 2008; Whitehouse & Colvin, 2001). Yet, the fact that most early childhood teachers come from socioeconomic, racial, cultural, and linguistic backgrounds which differ from the majority of their students' (Haddix, 2008; Zumwalt & Craig, 2005) makes such practices exclusionary. The challenge then is for teachers and schools to embrace more inclusive approaches, tools, and strategies in classrooms and (pre)schools.

## WAYS TO USE COMMUNITY RESOURCES AND HOME LITERACIES

Janice Baines, a 1st-grade teacher in Columbia, South Carolina, engages in home visits and community explorations as she gets to know the children she teaches, their homes, and communities. She pays particular attention to the history and practices of the communities in which the children live, bringing these learnings to the ways she teaches 1st grade. She brings together the academic demands of the 1st-grade curriculum with what the children already know—their home literacies and community resources. For example, in terms of environmental print, she brings community images to her classroom, thus showing her students that they already know how to read. She engages in supporting and fostering their oral language development through interviews (see also Chapter 3), resulting in writing the histories of their communities (which happen to be very rich, but may be missing from printed books). She listens to what they sing and brings the melody of known songs with new lyrics—developing "I Can Read Swag" from "Pretty Boy Swag."

Ms. Baines recognizes that children learn language and literacies at home and in communities, an approach significantly different from that of traditional emergent literacy scholars who define emergent literacy as the acquisition of skills necessary for reading and conceptualize home literacy practices as transitory "stepping stones" to be left behind when more traditional literacy practices develop (Souto-Manning, 2010c). Yet, Ms. Baines shows us that home literacies are not stepping stones to be left behind. They are not crutches to be cast off. They are real and meaningful culturally specific practices that shape many children's and adults' interactions and experiences. While Ms. Baines knows that children of color should be taught the power code (Mainstream American English), she understands that children have the right to continue developing home and community literacies alongside more traditional schooling practices thereby becoming full participants of different (and sometimes conflicting) contexts—such as home and school. Instead of seeking to colonize students or attempting to promote processes of erasure, teachers such as Ms. Baines see home languages and literacies as value-added literacy systems, as strengths. And while there are areas of overlap, these teachers believe that they must be aware of culturally specific rules that are separate across contexts—such as "guess-what-I-am-thinking" questions asked in didactic ways (Cazden, 1986), which are absent from the homes of many African American children (Heath, 1983).

Overall, employing community resources and home literacies to teach multiculturally is an approach resulting from a variety of tools and strategies—interviews and culture circles, for example. Such an approach can take place within the context of an inquiry—as long as the inquiry focuses on the communities of which the children are part and seeks to learn from and with their families about multiple literacies in practice across homes. It can involve storytelling and story acting (see Chapter 8), songwriting and singing. It can include technology (see Chapter 7). The ways of employing community resources and home literacies are many. As you enter Ms. Baines's 1st-grade classroom, I invite you to re-create, to reinvent ways to engage in honoring community resources and home literacies as you teach multiculturally in your own setting.

## GETTING STARTED

Home and community visits are essential for getting started—for learning about who your students are, the language and literacy practices present in their homes, and the cultural practices prevalent in their communities.

Instead of seeing students for what they do not have when they enter kindergarten or 1st grade (in terms of traditional school and literacy skills—letters, numbers, etc.), it is important to see what they do have, what they bring with them. In doing so, early childhood teachers can make connections that make teaching and learning more accessible and meaningful to all children.

Walking around communities and taking photos of places that are meaningful to the children is also important. These photos can serve as environmental print and are starting points for connections in the classroom; for example, a picture of Family Dollar, which may be familiar to Fabienne and happens to start with the same letter as her name. It is also important to take photos of things that are part of your life—especially when your students are familiar with these things. For example, the children may be familiar with a restaurant or grocery store you go to (even if they don't go there) or with the college you attended. These can help them connect with you as a human being. In addition to photos of places, it is important to have photos of common products (or packages). One example is Blue Magic, a common hair product for many African American children in Ms. Baines's classroom. Pictures of such familiar spaces and objects can make the classroom more welcoming.

As a teacher, you can use such pictures to make a community book and invite the children to engage in shared reading, showing them that they can indeed read. This book can initially be a picture book where children read graphic labels, pictures, and symbols. Later, word labels may be added. When they realize what they already know, they can then make connections which may lead to more traditional reading skills, such as letter-sound correspondence. It is thus important to start by showing children what they *can* do—while mediating traditional literacy skills with community resources. After all, children will more likely be able to read a book featuring known places, products, and people. According to Ms. Baines, taking this approach gives children the message that they already read—they just didn't know they could read. Taking the time to show them how capable they are is important—and such community and family connections are key.

Each year, Ms. Baines makes several books with her 1st-graders. One example of the kinds of books they make is a book about the community where the children live—with their insights, knowledge, and perspectives. They also make a book featuring each 1st-grade student as a unique individual, who is part of a group, of a community of learners. Then Ms. Baines uses these books—featuring knowledge the children already have—in shared readings, thereby showing the children how much each of them already knows. This enables some of the more reluctant readers to gain confidence and fluency as they pick up one of the class-made books featuring their communities again and again because they are familiar with its illustrations, words, and phrases. This is a great way to get started showing students that their experiences, practices, and knowledge outside of school really count in school. It is a great way to honor the community resources they bring to the classroom and to cast a positive, strengths-based light onto their practices.

Ms. Baines has also employed songs. It has been her practice to listen to the radio and learn the songs her students come into the classroom sing-ing—or that they sing at home and in their communities. This is how she found out about the popularity of "Pretty Boy Swag." She took advantage of their knowledge of the song, kept the melody, and wrote new words, ar-ranging a new version of "Pretty Boy Swag" entitled "I Can Read Swag." They sang these newly created songs with known melodies nonstop—at home, in the classroom, in the playground, etc.

To engage in powerful practices such as Ms. Baines's, it is important to start by looking closely and listening carefully to the voices and practices of the young children you teach. Listening to what children say is key—not only to what they are saying, but how they are talking. This is important as teachers can then make connections between students' home languages (African American Language, Spanish) and the school-privileged and sanc-tioned academic language (Mainstream American English), thus negotiating bridges of access with the children. We must consider serious and impor-tant issues such as the importance of understanding the validity of multiple languages and seeing those who are fluent speakers of African American Language and developing speakers of Mainstream American English as emergent bilinguals instead of seeing them as speaking broken languages, as not knowing English. While I do not expand on African American Language as a language here, if you have any questions about the myth of African American Language as a broken language or as wrong English, please refer to "Further Resources" at the end of this chapter.

## CONSIDERING OBSTACLES, EXPLORING POSSIBILITIES

The first obstacle to engaging in this kind of teaching may be dealing with the belief that home literacies and community resources do not fully ad-dress and satisfy the mandated standards and adopted curriculum. You can attend to this by clearly outlining the ways that you are addressing the standards in meaningful and authentic ways. In the example below, I make clear how Janice Baines employed community resources and home literacies to teach multiculturally while simultaneously supporting stu-dents with regard to the Common Core State Standards, specifically in the areas of Speaking and Listening. Making clear to administrators, col-leagues, and families how your teaching addresses these standards is key to overcoming this obstacle.

The second obstacle is comprised of misconceptions regarding home visits. It is essential to learn about the homes and communites in which your students live—and the literacy practices present in their homes (oral storytelling, hymns, etc.). Many may say that the neighborhoods and communities where the children live are dangerous. I challenge you to find the positives in the neighborhoods where your students live. Their communities are rich. Visit their homes if possible. Arrange with parents and family members ahead of time and ask about the best day and time to visit—as well as the best location. At first some families may prefer to meet at a community location—such as a grocery store or a church—until trust and a true relationship is developed. Don't sponsor negative views of the communities and families who are part of the lives of the children you teach. Learn with them, respect them, and appreciate their essential role in their children's lives. As Ms. Baines explains:

> Some may think of home and community visits as dangerous—but these are the places that the children we teach inhabit. If we cannot go there, what message are we sending the children? You have to go in with a different perspective. . . . No one is gonna bother you. They are gonna love you more! In each neighborhood that I visit, that they say is bad, I am greeted, I am recognized, and I am invited to eat dinner.

Finally, finding time to do this work can be challenging—especially considering paperwork and other demands. In trying to find time for home visits, it is important to focus on what is most important to the children you teach and prioritize accordingly. It is all about focusing on what is important to the children you are teaching instead of feeling pressed and oppressed by governmental demands and mandates. Once you find the time to get started, you will experience the greatest possibility in this kind of teaching. As you value each and every child and what he or she already knows and brings to the classroom, you will see them grow excited about their learning and confident in their abilities. Because you will be highlighting their strengths, the children you teach will feel better about themselves. They will feel better about learning—because it will be relevant to their lives outside of school. Finally, when you value family and community practices in your classroom you will give children and their families the message that you care about them (Heath, 2012).

## BRINGING COMMUNITY RESOURCES AND HOME LITERACIES INTO AN EARLY CHILDHOOD SETTING

What does an early childhood classroom look like when a teacher uses community resources and home literacies to develop funds of knowledge and teach multiculturally? While there are many ways of teaching which honor the communities where children live and build on their home literacies, here I invite you to enter Janice Baines's 1st-grade classroom in Columbia, South Carolina, and learn how community resources and home literacies came to life in her 1st grade. Let's begin by learning more about the teacher and the school where she teaches.

## The Teacher

Janice Baines is a 1st-grade teacher at Carver-Lyon Elementary School in Columbia, SC. All of the students at Carver-Lyon Elementary are African American. The school has a rate of free and/or reduced lunch of over 90%. In addition, the school is a Title I school designated under appropriate state and federal regulations. Carver-Lyon Elementary is located in an African American community listed on the National Register of Historic Places. While there are rich histories, legacies, and cultural practices in the community, most of the media portrayals of the community are from a deficit prospective, highlighting crimes, gang activity, poverty, and unemployment.

Ms. Baines has been teaching 1st grade at Carver-Lyon Elementary for 6 years. Prior to being a 1st-grade teacher, Ms. Baines taught toddlers in a preschool in Columbia, SC. A graduate of Benedict College, a historically Black college, she now works closely with Professor Susi Long at the University of South Carolina as she seeks to better educate young children in culturally responsive ways. Along with another Carver-Lyon Elementary School teacher, Carmen Tisdale, Ms. Baines is part of a teacher study group committed to educational equity. Over the years she's seen how powerful it is to teach in a way that honors children's home literacies and community resources.

As an African American teacher teaching African American children, Ms. Baines took the opportunity to spend a month in 2011 in Sierra Leone as part of a Fulbright-Hayes scholarship program to learn about connections between education in South Carolina and education in what she calls "Africa, my motherland, my home." By doing so, she expanded notions of home and community in historical ways—considering issues of forced immigration, of slavery. Ms. Baines believes once African American children know who they are within their immediate community, it is important for them to go global and understand that Africa is their motherland.

## The Classroom

Where are you from? What is your history? As with many historically Black places in the United States, there were no books that portrayed the richness of the community where Janice Baines's 1st-graders lived. Yet, Ms. Baines wanted to honor and positively portray the many resources available in the community so important to the children she taught. She decided to create books through an oral history and exploration of the Waverly community—the community where her students lived. She came to learn about the multiple communities (within the Waverly community) of which the children were members—their families, the churches of which they were a part (12 in total), as well as the barbershop and the community hospital. Ms. Baines employed a wealth of community resources and home literacies to create bridges that connected the children's out-of-school lives with their in-school lives. She wanted them to see themselves as inherent and valuable members of her 1st grade, in spite of the Eurocentric curricula and standards that tend to exclude children of color.

She committed to learning with the students about their communities. In this learning journey, she blurred the roles of teacher and learner and learned much about the communities in which the children lived. For example, she uncovered the history of a 40-year-old barbershop that served many of the children and their extended families. To make that process visible and fashion a curriculum from the rich community threads, Ms. Baines organized interviews to document the history of this barbershop within their community—a significant community hub—a place for African American males to put down all their problems, learn different things, and so much more.

In putting the barbershop at the center of her curriculum and teaching, Ms. Baines started making visible many of the powerful practices that went on in everyday settings—bridging familiar places and practices with school skills and knowledge. The children came to understand the many learning opportunities which took place in that barbershop. That barbershop had been a place for learning—a space that valued community resources, home literacies, and individual histories—for decades. Ms. Baines was able to connect the barbershop not only to developing and supporting oral language through interviews and writing a book in the context of the Waverly community, but also engaged her students in reading about the significance of barbershops to African American communities throughout the country. In addition, Ms. Baines drew on the barbershop to teach about money, problem-solving, and strategy. For example, there was a chessboard in the barbershop which led children to want to learn about chess—thereby learning to strategize and problem-solve. Because there was a chessboard in a familiar place, the children did not see it as school-related literacy, but as a known, accessible game. Without even realizing, the children were engaging in mathematics—considering the cost of barbershop services, calculating change (by adding to and by subtracting from)—and strategizing through a game of chess.

In addition to learning about and from the barbershop, its history, practices, and importance, Ms. Baines also created opportunities for the children to learn from and about people they saw every day. One of those people was Ms. Myers, a school custodian who had grown up in the Waverly community. In preparing the children to interview Ms. Myers, Ms. Baines told them that they should ask questions that would lead to learning about the person's story, where the person lived, what the person thought, and who the person was. She told the children to think about the questions in a way that would enable them to write a book about that person. Ms. Baines asked the children: "So—what questions would you ask her?" The children took the task at hand very seriously. They developed and asked questions and learned through them. Some of the questions were: What did you do when you were a young girl? What school did you go to? What did the neighborhood look like when you were growing up? How is it different from today? How is it similar? If you could change anything about the neighborhood, what would it be? What is the neighborhood's biggest treasure? Why?

As they engaged in this learning journey, the children developed interview and research skills, part of the 1st-grade curriculum and standards. Specifically, one of the 1st-grade standards is to develop how and why questions. The children in Ms. Baines's 1st-grade classroom were able to not only develop, but also to test and revise meaningful and authentic questions. They also moved beyond standards, developing questions leading to inferences—what if?, for example. In seeking to delve deeper, the children asked vocabulary questions, questions related to literal and inferential comprehension, and analytical questions. In asking the questions they designed, they learned about their community by interviewing Ms. Myers and by listening to her amazing stories. They learned that as a child Ms. Myers had attended the same school they did—Carver-Lyon Elementary School.

Ms. Myers helped the children understand the rich history of the community as well as the issues caused by the more recent gentrification of the neighborhood (Kinloch, 2010). In studying about the gentrification of their community, they started discussing issues of fairness, segregation, and exclusion on the basis of race, gender, education, and income. Together, they looked at issues of fairness and exclusion historically on a national level and read about Martin Luther King Jr. and about Rosa Parks—*Martin's Big Words: The Life of Dr. Martin Luther King, Jr.* (Rappaport & Collier, 2001) and *Rosa* (Giovanni, 2005). As they considered the history of their community, they considered how people in the community were being displaced by gentrification efforts and problematized the renaming of gentrified sections of their community. With the children she taught, Ms. Baines was committed to exploring what was going on in their community at the time, the history and the face of the community before, as well as how and why it had changed. Ms. Baines wanted to learn with the children about what made their community so special.

In addition to researching specific locations and people through interviews, Ms. Baines took the children across the community. Together, they took pictures of important and meaningful locations—from the perspective of children who were simultaneously members of the classroom and of the Waverly community. Ms. Baines invited the children to bring artifacts to the classroom. She took pictures of them, creating a visual history of the community resources and home literacies available—making many of the invisible and taken-for-granted practices of children's homes and communities visible and acknowledged within the context of the classroom. In addition, the children documented their community resources and home literacies through drawings. These photos and drawings became illustrations for class-made books about the community. And the text that went along with the pictures featured developed from the children's perspectives of what they saw and how they remembered objects, places, and people featured in them. The books portrayed the children's insights, questions, and ways of making sense of their worlds through photos, drawings, and words.

Beyond learning about their own community's history and writing books about the community, Ms. Baines and her students named the Whiteness of so many traditional children's books. As a community of learners, they rewrote those stories, locating them within the community where they lived, casting African American characters, and using more common details (for example, *Goldilocks* was retitled *Star Braid and the Three Bears*; Star Braid ate grits instead of porridge). This seemingly simple act challenged the Eurocentric nature of so many common stories—such as *Goldilocks and the Three Bears*, *Cinderella*, *Little Red Riding Hood*, etc. In addition to revising traditional stories, making them more inclusive and representative, Ms. Baines constantly brought books that featured a variety of African American leaders and histories to her classroom, making visible the many possibilities that would become part of the children's future.

In terms of languages, in Ms. Baines's classroom the children had the freedom to write and talk in African American Language or whatever language they chose. At the beginning of each year, Ms. Baines has a habit of introducing languages and language use very clearly—discussing the different languages and registers present in the classroom community. She said:

> There are at least two ways that we are going to talk in here—there is the school way of talking and there is the home way of talking [African American Language]. But even the home way of talking can be different. The way that I talk when I am at home, at a party, or a cookout may be similar to the way you talk. But I may say some things that no one else says. At school, they say that because there may be some people from China or Brazil or anywhere in the world that we need to speak the same. We need to talk the school way. As long as you know how to speak school and how to speak home, and know that they are different, you can choose the language you want.

Ms. Baines highlights this awareness so that the children will switch languages in the classroom, according to interlocutor (teacher, principal, peer), context (playground, circle time, centers), and medium (oral, written). Ms. Baines talks about code-switching upfront, when she first meets her students, as she wants them to develop Mainstream American English while feeling confident in their fluency in African American Language. From then on, the children talk about language practices with more openness as they are aware of the possibilities of code-switching and are not ashamed of speaking African American Language. Ms. Baines talks about her students' home language practices as valid and full—doing away with any idea of fixing them.

She underlines that to engage in this kind of teaching, every teacher needs to know the standards well and make visible how the standards are addressed through the use of home literacies and community resources. Figure 6.1 shows some of the standards Ms. Baines addressed as she engaged in the learning journey portrayed above. And these are just a few of many more standards addressed by Ms. Baines in her 1st-grade classroom while using community resources and home literacies to teach in multicultural and culturally relevant ways (restricted to the area of Speaking and Listening here for illustration purposes only; see also Long, 2011—Chapter 3 features Ms. Baines's teaching).

**Figure 6.1. Common Core State Standards, Speaking and Listening**

Standard SL 1.1. Participate in collaborative conversations with diverse partners about grade 1 topics and texts with peers and adults in small and larger groups.

Standard SL 1.2. Ask and answer questions about key details in a text read aloud or information presented orally or through other media.

Standard SL 1.3. Ask and answer questions about what a speaker says in order to gather additional information or to clarify something that is not understood.

Source: Long, 2011, p. 54

## The Teacher's Perspective

Home visits are key to the teaching in which Janice Baines engages. She says:

> Why conduct home visits? Because you know that it is the only way you will see that parent who is working two jobs, that parent who has no transportation, that parent who has little ones and no childcare, or that parent who may really feel intimidated about or inadequate

coming to school. Because it is the only way that parents will know that you as a teacher truly care about their child and are ready to work on his or her behalf. Because it is a time for establishing real relationships—and showing families that you truly value them and want them engaged in a partnership to advantage their child. Because it is a wonderful learning opportunity!

While home visits are not mandatory at Carver-Lyon Elementary School, Ms. Baines is committed to them and does them at the beginning of each school year. To show trust, while Ms. Baines does not invite each of the families to her home, she gives the parents her cell phone number—so that there is an open line of communication and so they feel that they can reach her when they need to. At times, she receives calls after traumatic events happen and she appreciates them as she can prepare and try to make the child's day better. Other times, she may get a call explaining that the child did not sleep well. Ms. Baines cares and wants to know about her students' home lives. And she wants the families to know that she trusts them—giving them her cell phone number is a small token of this trust.

Be respectful of the families, and schedule the home visits at their convenience. If parents want you to come at a certain time or day of the week, they often have a reason. Don't question them; just show your respect and appreciation for the opportunity by making arrangements to conduct the home visits when it is most convenient for the families.

Ms. Baines advises teachers who are considering doing this work and engaging in learning from children's homes and communities:

> You cannot go in with negative views already. You have no business teaching if you cannot do away with negative views of the children whom you teach (which include their homes, families, and communities). As a teacher, go in and introduce yourself. Ask them how they are doing and share with them that together you can work on behalf of their child. Be honest.

During home visits, Ms. Baines outlines the learning opportunities she sees. She highlights the positives: "Oh, great, you have lots of reading around here. I see *Jet* magazine and I see a Bible." She recounts: "I tell them about all the learning that is already going on in their home so that they are aware of the many wonderful things they are already doing. It is important not to give parents messages that something is wrong with their home."

## REFLECTING ON COMMUNITY RESOURCES AND HOME LITERACIES AS TOOLS FOR TEACHING MULTICULTURALLY

When you make home visits, it is important to remain positive, to describe what you see as opposed to comparing any family's practices to your own—as if your family practices were a criterion against which all other families were measured. So, before you go to a child's home, prepare yourself to learn—and not to judge. Further, value home literacies by bringing literacy practices from children's homes to the school.

As a teacher, you may come to learn that school has not always been a welcoming place to parents and family members of traditionally minoritized children. So, it is important to show adult family members that your classroom is different and how you value their practices—and show your commitment to make their children's educational experience better, more positive than theirs may have been. Furthermore, it is important to let them know that you are not trying to replace them or to judge their practices, but that you need them in order to more fully and successfully teach their child. This approach will develop authentic and purposeful partnerships. Together, teachers and families can make commitments to not only love but to care about and for each child (Heath, 2012)—to engage in actions that will honor each child and help him or her develop so that he or she can envision the many possibilities that lay ahead. In this way, you are continuing to honor where students come from and the multiple communities of which they are members.

## FURTHER RESOURCES

Allen, J. (2007). *Creating welcoming schools: A practical guide to home-school partnerships with diverse families.* New York: Teachers College Press.

Gonzalez, N., Moll, L. C., & Amanti, C. (2005). *Funds of knowledge: Theorizing practices in households and classrooms.* Mahwah, NJ: Lawrence Erlbaum Associates.

Gregory, E., Long, S., & Volk, D. (Eds). (2004). *Many pathways to literacy: Young children learning with siblings, peers, grandparents, and communities.* London, UK: RoutledgeFalmer.

Kinloch, V. (2010). *Harlem on our minds: Place, race, and the literacies of urban youth.* New York: Teachers College Press.

Ladson-Billings, G. (1994). *The dreamkeepers: Successful teachers of African American children.* San Francisco: Jossey-Bass Publishers.

Long, S. (2011). *Supporting students in a time of core standards: English language arts grades PreK–2.* Urbana, IL: National Council of Teachers of English.

Nieto, S. (1999). *The light in their eyes: Creating multicultural learning communities.* New York: Teachers College Press.

## On African American Language

Delpit, L., & Dowdy, J. K. (Eds.). (2002). *The skin that we speak: Thoughts on language and culture in the classroom*. New York: The New Press.
Macneil/Lehrer Productions. (2005). *Do you speak American? From sea to shining sea: English varieties, African American English*. http://www.pbs.org/speak/seatosea/americanvarieties/AAVE/
Rickford, J. R., & Rickford, R. J. (2000). *Spoken soul: The story of Black English*. New York: Wiley.
Smitherman, G. (2006). *Word from the mother: Language and African Americans*. New York: Routledge.

# CHAPTER 7

# Technology:
# Media(ting) Multicultural Teaching

"Google it," "text her," and "email him" are common expressions used by adults and children in the 21st century. Young children may ask teachers to document their learnings via digital pictures. Then, they may want to look at the digital picture immediately and even request that picture be sent to a family member electronically. Technology can thus mediate home and school in ways that invite families to learn about their children in school. Technology has become a way of communicating across time and space. In many early childhood classrooms, children pretend to play on computers and talk on cell phones. At home, they may communicate with relatives across geographic and language borders via Skype or FaceTime. While the specific technologies employed by young children and their families are likely to change over time, the role of technology in communicating is likely to remain paramount, shaping the lives of the children we teach.

In fact, it has been said that young children are "digital natives" (Palfrey & Gasser, 2010). We teachers who are often digital immigrants need to honor the digital natives we teach. We have the obligation to learn to use technology in our teaching in ways that make education more multicultural and equitable. There are many ways to do so. In this chapter, I explain the use of technology to mediate multicultural education. In doing so, we meet Dahlia Bouari, a kindergarten teacher at P.S. 89 in New York City, and her practice of blogging as a way of documenting children's learnings, communicating authentically, and strengthening connections with families. In addition, we enter a 2nd-grade classroom in Falls Church, Virginia, where Carol Felderman and her students engaged in podcasting. In both of these settings, technology is used to mediate more equitable educational practices.

## WHY TECHNOLOGY AS A TOOL FOR
## MEDIATING MULTICULTURAL TEACHING?

Technology can serve as a powerful tool for multicultural education. As discussed earlier, the transformation of curriculum and teaching and the transformation of society are important goals of multicultural education (Gorski, 2010b). Through the use of technology, the transformation of the curriculum and teaching that goes on in classrooms can reach beyond the classroom walls, informing families, communities, classrooms, and (pre) schools known and unknown to the specific community of learners.

Technology can be a tool for teaching multiculturally because it can illuminate the ways in which (pre)schools can be restructured to be more inclusive, equitable, and empowering (Banks, 2007). Multicultural education focuses on action and empowers students, teachers, schools, and communities to become social justice activists (Grant & Sleeter, 2007). Technology serves as a tool for the empowerment of students and teachers across time and space, thus disseminating transformative actions and influencing schools and communities both near and far.

## WAYS TO USE TECHNOLOGY

Technology is a tool that can be employed to mediate multicultural education within any given strategy or approach. So, whether you are engaging in inquiry, interviews, culture circles, storytelling and story acting, community resources and home literacies, or plan to use these or any other approach, tool, or strategy for teaching young children multiculturally in the future, you can productively employ technology, thus enhancing the power of the practices that go on in your classroom.

Dahlia Bouari (or Dahlia as her kindergartners call her) started using technology in her first year of teaching to communicate with the families of the children with whom she learns and teaches. She created a password-protected blog where she displays children's learning journeys as well as their points of view and perspectives on a variety of topics through stories, pictures, drawings, and audio files. The blog serves as a way of communicating with families, but also as a way of virtually inviting families into the classroom—keeping them apprised of the classroom happenings. Through the blog, Dahlia invites family members to offer their own perspectives and experiences, which are then brought to her curriculum and teaching. While she notes that access is an issue, she finds that her teaching is richer because of technology, which mediates a variety of home and school spaces inhabited by the children she teaches.

Carol Felderman employed technology to mediate communication not only with the families of the children she taught, but also with the world at large through the *100% Kids Podcast*, an on-demand Internet-based audio broadcasting show organized into episodes (see Figure 7.1). According to the website (http://www.bazmakaz.com/100kids/about/):

> This is a show created by a group of second graders with their teacher Carol Felderman and their friend Vivian Vasquez from American

**Figure 7.1. 100% Kids**

*Source:* http://www.bazmakaz.com/100kids/2007 by Vivian Vasquez

University. They started the podcast as a way to create space to talk about ways in which they are working to help make the world a better place for all.

They are called podcasts because these audio broadcasts are often listened to on mobile devices such as iPods. They are easily accessible and can be streamed or downloaded. The children in Mrs. Felderman's 2nd grade used podcasts to recount their learning journeys, putting together one podcast each week. They made access to their podcasts public by securing permission from families and using special podcast names (pseudonyms) for each child. Many of their podcasts have been accessed by hundreds of people throughout the world (as indicated by ClustrMaps, a software that tracks the location and number of accesses on a world map). More on Carol Felderman's use of podcasts is presented later in this chapter.

Overall, technology can serve as a tool for mediating homes, schools, and communities and for making visible the powerful actions going on in specific classrooms. Technology can open up the silos of classrooms and create a bigger conversation on the possibilities of teaching for equity and transformation. Technology can serve as a tool for envisioning vast new possibilities—across time and space.

## GETTING STARTED

Carol Felderman has vowed to take on a new challenge each year as the children she teaches take on many. She always focuses on a challenge with the potential to improve her teaching. Technology had always been a challenge for Carol Felderman, but one year, she decided to tackle that challenge. The idea of technology as a welcome challenge came from the children Mrs. Felderman taught as she reflected on her previous year of teaching and realized how much technology was part of her students' lives. Previously, Mrs. Felderman tended to resort to the overhead projector as her technology of choice in the classroom. Thus, to get started she embraced and welcomed the unknown.

Blurring the roles of teacher and learner and unsettling traditional power dynamics in the classroom are important parts of getting started—realizing that many times the children may know more than you do. In embracing the unknown, being honest with children is essential. Mrs. Felderman recounts the children's shock when she said: "I am learning. I don't know everything." In addition to being honest about what you know, you need to know what resources you have. Finally, Mrs. Felderman underlined: "Having the support of a community of teacher-learners was essential." As teachers came together to talk about their practices, Mrs. Felderman was able to negotiate the challenges she experienced. It was also important to realize that sometimes things may not work as they should, but as Mrs. Felderman states, "Keep going after those scary things and recruit help."

Here are some thoughts as you consider getting started using technology as a tool to mediate multicultural education:

- Learn as you engage in this journey—
  don't wait until you know it all.
- Assess what you have and identify what you need.
- Recruit help—of other teachers, of professors or
  researchers that may be accessible to you, of former
  students, and of students' family members.

As Mrs. Felderman declared: "No one knows everything there is to know. So I had to give it a try—just like I asked my kids to give it a try every day. I took on the invitation I issued every day—to learn." And be honest with yourself. Dahlia Bouari stated: "I want to improve!" Don't we all? We want to improve not only our use of technology, but our teaching practices as well.

## CONSIDERING OBSTACLES, EXPLORING POSSIBILITIES

I invite you to stop and think about some of the obstacles and possibilities of employing technology as a tool for mediating multicultural teaching in your own setting. As outlined below, there are many potential obstacles to using technology—limited family accessibility, restricted time to use technology (especially in light of today's demands and pressures on teachers), lack of technological expertise, and minimal resources. Yet, I hope you will find that the possibilities of using technology to mediate multicultural education far outweigh such obstacles.

## Limited Family Accessibility

One of the obstacles of using technology to mediate multicultural teaching is that of accessibility. How can you do this kind of work without excluding families? Dahlia Bouari is negotiating ways of making her blog more accessible to families in her classroom community. While some families access the blog on a regular basis, others don't. And although there are computers available in her classroom, and she welcomes parents into her classroom, the network available in NYC public schools does not allow access to the blog she constructed. So, using a class blog can be a challenge. Partnering with public libraries or making the blog mobile device–friendly are two possible solutions. Carol Felderman attended to issues of access very early and very consciously. She made CDs of the podcasts available to every family. So, families that did not have access to computers or to the Internet at home were still able to listen to the podcasts produced by listening to a CD. In addition, Mrs. Felderman established an open door policy where family members were able to come in at any time to listen to the podcasts with their child. Yet, the issue of language access and inclusivity was one with which Mrs. Felderman wrestled. Parents and family members worked on translating some of the podcast episodes into Spanish. Nevertheless, because there were many more languages represented in her class, and while they made progress toward having bilingual podcasts—in English and Spanish—other languages were not represented.

## Restrictions of Schedule

Another challenge is finding time to engage in this work—using technology as a tool for teaching multiculturally. Mrs. Felderman found wiggle room in her schedule by transforming writing workshop time into a time to write podcast scripts. Reading time was transformed into a time to practice reading scripts, or to research materials for the show. "Recognizing the cross-curricular work that was part of putting together a show helped Carol not limit the amount of time crafting the scripts. Some days she and her students worked for 30 minutes and other days they spent the whole morning researching, writing, and revising" (Vasquez, 2010, p. 117). While this required some pedagogical imagination, Mrs. Feldman worked within the constraints of a Title I school and met mandated state standards across the following content areas: oral language, reading, and writing; science; math; social studies; and technology research tools. Although the standards may initially seem to be an obstacle, here I recast them as an advantage of this work.

## Lack of Technological Expertise

Another obstacle may be the teacher's lack of familiarity with the technology available. Embracing the learning journey is important here. As you read earlier, Mrs. Felderman was not familiar with technology beyond an overhead projector, but she took on the challenge and made her learning journey visible to the children she taught. Mrs. Felderman decided on podcasts after sharing a podcast with her 2nd-graders and seeing their excitement regarding podcasts. So, the podcasts emanated from the children's interests. As Mrs. Felderman said: "It's their learning—and if they are not interested in it, it's going to be my project. It needed to be their project. And it is exactly what it was." Although she had never put a podcast together before and did not know where to start, she decided she'd give it a try.

## Minimal Resources

Finally, one of the biggest obstacles is the availability of resources. In many classrooms throughout the country, there may be lots of contemporary technology (SMART boards, iPads, laptop computers, Internet, etc.). In others, there may be very little (a digital camera) or even none. Assessing the resources available and seeking to identify the key elements to using technology as a tool for teaching multiculturally is important. Once these resources are identified, you can recruit the help of administrators, families, other teachers, and related professionals (such as university professors) to get what you need. You may solicit donations of used technology from the school community or solicit resources via non-profit organizations such as Donors Choose (http://www.donorschoose.org/). You can also access the school library or media center, a public library, or a computer lab.

## Opportunities Offered

The obstacles to using technology in your classroom notwithstanding, think about the opportunities it offers to do the following:

- Combine children's love of technology
  with curriculum and standards;
- Incite children to become truly interested in writing
  because they know that their communication
  is real and authentic (Lindfors, 2008);
- Make the classroom-learning journey public to the world;
- Get children really interested in geography because
  they know that someone in Australia is listening
  to their podcasts or accessing their blog;

- Encourage children's interest in reading and valuing multiple languages because they know that their fluency matters and that multiple languages are needed to communicate with a multicultural and multilingual world;
- Reach families across geographic borders so that they can be involved in their children's education.

These are just a few examples of the possibilities afforded by technology as a tool for mediating multicultural education.

## BRINGING TECHNOLOGY INTO AN EARLY CHILDHOOD SETTING

What does an early childhood classroom look like when a teacher uses technology to mediate multicultural education? While there are many ways of using technology to mediate multicultural education, here I invite you to enter Carol Felderman's 2nd-grade classroom, listen to her students, and learn about how technology became a very important part of teaching for equity. In doing so, you will see how young children engaged in actions which resulted in change. Let's begin by learning about the teacher.

### The Teacher

Carol Branigan Felderman was a 2nd-grade teacher at Bailey's Elementary School for the Arts and Sciences in Falls Church, Virginia. She is a career changer who earned a master's degree leading to initial certification through classes offered at night. Her final student teaching was at Bailey's, which has around 1,000 students in kindergarten through 5th grade and is located in the Washington, DC, metropolitan area. Over 59% of its students are English language learners, 15% have identified special needs, and 63% qualify for free and/or reduced cost lunch. The demographics of its students are 56% Latino/a, 24.5% White, 11.5% Asian/Asian American, 4.5% African American, and 3.5% other racial and ethnic backgrounds.

As she started teaching at Bailey's in 2001, Mrs. Felderman learned about the many professional inquiry opportunities available. Bailey's was a school where teachers were always reading books, documenting their practices, and trying to make their teaching better. Mrs. Felderman recounts having some of her biggest learning experiences at Bailey's Elementary. It was the first place where she spent many hours as the only White person in the room (when she was teaching), which was very different from her experience growing up in Connecticut. "It opened my eyes to . . . the fact that I had to own my culture—and trouble it too. . . . Then, I was able to value the experiences the children were bringing," said Carol Felderman.

She sees her mission as a teacher to build a community of learners in which all are respectful and appreciative of each other's uniqueness. Mrs. Felderman says, "My mission is to have children challenge the privileges associated with certain identities, to race, class, gender, in society. To create a socially just community in our classroom where we understand that we are individuals and we are part of a community at the same time."

## The Classroom

Traditionally, each year all 2nd-graders at Bailey's Elementary School went to the Baltimore National Aquarium. However, in 2006–2007, the downturn of the U.S. economy resulted in school budget cuts. Although the 2nd-graders were excited about the trip of their lifetimes—one they'd been talking about since they entered the school—the principal realized that there was no money for the Baltimore Aquarium trip that year.

It was the second or third day of school when one of Mrs. Felderman's 2nd-graders asked her: "Are we going?" She responded: "No, we are not. We don't have enough money this year." Jovani chimed in: "That is not fair, you know, because my cousin and my brother went." Every 2nd grade they'd known had gone on that trip before—and now they couldn't go. "Why?" Yavette asked. Malik responded: "Well, the principal said we can't go. We can't go."

The children in Mrs. Felderman's 2nd-grade classroom were not happy and wanted to do something about this. They were not satisfied with Malik's rationalization that if the principal said they couldn't go, that was it. They started saying how they did not agree with the principal. Carolina summarized: "This is not fair! Maybe there is a way." The children approached this as an issue of fairness and tried to find ways to make the trip happen. Yaritza said: "It's about money, right? What if we can get the money?" "Let's ask!" said Ibrahim. This kicked off a grand exploration. The children had identified an unfair issue and wanted to question the issue, moving toward fashioning change collectively. Together, they talked about ways to discuss things that they didn't agree with. The children wrote and sent a letter to the principal asking if they could have a meeting with him. Upon hearing a positive response to their invitation, the children prepared for the meeting.

The principal came to the meeting in their classroom, and the children explained that they were interested in making the Baltimore Aquarium trip happen. They presented their ideas and expressed their feelings to the principal about how unfair this decision was. They suggested that they could sell cookies and lemonade to get started raising money for the trip. The principal said that he was intrigued by the conversation, as he had not thought about the trip to the Baltimore Aquarium as an issue of equity, but something that the school could not afford that year. Before he left, he said: "See what you can do. On my end, I will see what I can do." The meeting was successful and the children were happy to get feedback from him. The principal said: "I was there to listen. And I was impressed by how well the children were able to express themselves." Carol Felderman recounts his respect for the children: "He came in with a notepad, wrote down the children's concerns, and considered them seriously. It was a very serious meeting."

As they moved ahead, the children documented their learning journey via an audit trail (Vasquez, 2004; see Figure 7.2). This audit trail then served as material for a podcast, which recounted the children's quest for equity.

The children in Mrs. Felderman's 2nd-grade class also considered the other 2nd-graders in the school. As Asma asked: "Do they agree and want to go?" Mrs. Felderman introduced them to the idea of a petition—explaining what a petition is, what it means to sign one, etc. In seeking to answer Asma's question, the children designed a petition to gather this information. By signing the petition that Mrs. Felderman's 2nd-graders had authored, other 2nd-graders would indicate that they also wanted to go to the Baltimore Aquarium. In pairs, the children presented the petition in English and Spanish to the other 2nd-grade classes, inviting the students to sign it. Mrs. Felderman's 2nd-graders explained to their peers what a petition is, what they were going to do with it, its purpose, and made sure that all 2nd-graders understood the petition. As they presented the petition, they learned that while some of the children at Bailey's Elementary would have

Figure 7.2. Audit Trail Documenting Learning Journey

been able to visit the Baltimore Aquarium with their families if the school trip had not taken place, many indicated that distance and cost made the trip prohibitive. This further fueled Mrs. Felderman's 2nd-graders to help everyone access the Baltimore Aquarium. After gathering signatures, Mrs. Felderman's 2nd-graders gave the petition to the principal—signed by every 2nd-grade student at Bailey's.

Partly due to the children's fundraising efforts, partly due to the principal's awareness of how important the trip was to the 2nd-graders, and partly due to PTA support, the children in all eight 2nd-grade classrooms at Bailey's Elementary School were able to go the Baltimore Aquarium that year. The children felt that this was such a wonderful accomplishment that they wanted to share their journey with the world in a podcast entitled: "We did it and so can you!" In this podcast, they invite others to engage in collective actions that seek to challenge injustices such as the one they experienced—the socioeconomic exclusion of children who would not have been able to go to the aquarium due to administrative efforts to balance the school budget. While I encourage you to listen to the podcast in its entirety, the following is a glimpse of their show, which has been downloaded around 2,000 times since 2007.

**100% KIDS!**

Hi! My name is Izzy and we raised enough money to go to the Baltimore Aquarium and we still have leftover money and we went to the Baltimore Aquarium on May 8. We sold pizza, water, soda, and popcorn and crafts.

Hi! I'm Kia. We went to the Baltimore Aquarium! That's what we did on May 8th, Tuesday. . . . Our class finally got the whole second grade to go to the Baltimore Aquarium. I think it's amazing how a bunch of 2nd-graders got all the second graders in our school to go to the Baltimore Aquarium. It's all so wonderful. Bye! And remember, I'm Kia.

Hi! My name is Lucy. I worked so hard to go to the Baltimore Aquarium. Not just me, the whole class tried to raise money to go to the Baltimore Aquarium. And we did it and I am so proud! Bye! And remember, I'm Lucy.

Hi! I'm Aman. I think that we should contact the Guinness Book of World Records because we paid for our field trip to the Baltimore Aquarium. The way we did it was selling items, for example, we sold crafts and pizza. Bye!

Hi! It's me, Scarlett. I'm back again. We did it! We went to the Baltimore Aquarium. We were working on this since the beginning of the year and now it's our last field trip of the year, we are almost done with the whole school year. There is only like one and a half or less months to go...where finally 3rd grade is. There is not much to say but the only thing I can say is "How?" because I can't really understand how we did all that to go to the Baltimore Aquarium. It's just so confusing how we did it. And we brought the trip back to 2nd grade!

Hi! My name is Danny . . . almost all of us worked on bingo night even though I wasn't there, but I know that we raised a lot of money . . . and we got to take the trip. And I thank Ms. Armando's class a lot for helping us go to the trip.

This is it! We did it. Woohooo!

Hi! My name is Miles. I liked going to the Baltimore Aquarium, and I got to sell pizza, and today we had a pizza party.

Hi! My name is Zach and I'm glad I got to go to the Baltimore Aquarium, and I sold pizza.

Hi! My name is Kelly, and on May 8 we went to the Baltimore Aquarium. It was fun. We got to see a whole bunch of animals. Let me tell you something. My teacher says that we would not go to the Baltimore Aquarium because we didn't have enough money to go, but we did. We proved her wrong. We are right. . . .

Hi! I'm Sabina, and on May 8th we went to the Baltimore Aquarium. We raised money, we sell the popcorns and pizza. And when we went inside the Baltimore Aquarium it was *cool* and awesome!

¡Hola! Mi nombre es Kéli. Yo quiero decirle algo. Yo, los otros fuimos en un paseo llamar el Baltimore Aquarium. Era divertido. Le voy a decir algo. Mi maestra dijo que no pudemos a ir porque no tenemos mucho dinero. Pero mis compañeros dicieron que sí, que pudemos a ir. Y mire que pasó. Sí, podemos a ir. Ella lo dijo muy mal.

Then, the children sang together a modified version of Ben Harper's "With My Own Two Hands":

I can change the world with my own two hands. Make it a better place with my own two hands. . . . I can reach out to you with my

own two hands. . . . Make it a better place with my own two hands.
. . . I'm gonna help the human race with my own two hands. . . . I
can comfort you with my own two hands. . . . But you got to use . . .
your own two hands. . . .

And then, all together, the children cheered and declared: *"We did it! And
so can you!"*

## The Teacher's Perspective

From Mrs. Felderman's perspective, it really comes down to introducing
technology as tools to the children. She reminds us that the important work
is not about podcasts per se, but about using the technology available to
mediate multicultural education, to get it to transcend the classroom walls
and engage with the larger community. Podcasts were the best technology
for Mrs. Felderman and her 2nd-graders at the time, but it may not be the
best technology available to mediate multicultural education in classrooms
of teachers who are starting now. Mrs. Felderman advises:

> Now podcasts are a thing of the past—so check and see what tools
> are available. Now I see teachers with Twitter accounts for their kids,
> communicating their classroom actions to a wide audience worldwide.
> . . . And other teachers use Skype to get their kids to talk with people
> who are really far away, contributing to their learning in really
> incredible ways.

Employing podcasts as tools, each week Mrs. Felderman and her 2nd-
graders engaged in a similar process, which involved reflection on the previous learnings broadcasted beyond the classroom walls and plans for future
broadcasts. Mrs. Felderman explains: "On Monday, they would reflect on
our previous show, which would have been posted on that previous Friday.
During our class meeting, we would talk about the show. And then we
would brainstorm topics for the week's show."

Carol Felderman invites us to focus not only on putting things out
there via technology, but to take the time to reflect on the podcasts, on
the Tweets, on any technological tools we use. Did they work the way we
wanted? What responses did we receive? Do we need to reconsider what
we are doing? How do we move ahead? These are all questions that Mrs.
Felderman considered in reflecting on the podcasts she and her students
produced. But these can also be questions employed when reflecting on any
technology employed.

The *100% Kids* podcasts not only transcended the classroom walls, but
geographic borders in the world map. There were many immigrant families

at Bailey's Elementary School, and many of these families were transnational (part living in the United States and part living in countries such as Mexico and Colombia). Through podcasts, Mrs. Felderman engaged transnational families. Family members who were geographically apart from the children were able to listen to the podcasts and remain connected to their child's learning journey even if from a geographically distant location. For example, the mother of a girl in Mrs. Felderman's class said: "My parents can listen to their granddaughter, in Colombia. They go to the Internet café every weekend to listen to her and learn about what she is doing." Mrs. Felderman herself recounts: "The summer after, I knew that some families had gone back to their home countries and I saw dots go up on the map [in ClustrMaps] as the children accessed the podcasts. When a dot went up in Saudi Arabia, I thought 'I know exactly who is listening over there.'"

Beyond their families, the children became interested in learning locations where people were accessing their podcasts. Through ClustrMaps and Google Analytics they tracked accesses in terms of geographic locations and languages. These tools offered wonderful learning opportunities and connections to the 2nd-grade social studies curriculum—expanding the practice of talking about where the children were from, and also creating connections to specific places that appeared on their ClustrMaps (see www.clustrmaps.com/).

These practices also led to an awareness of language access as an issue of fairness. At one point, the children wanted the podcasts to be in the seven different languages identified according to Google Analytics information. They realized that while they were engaging in more inclusive and equitable practices, their podcasts were not fully inclusive. Yet, they decided to take small steps and instead of translating the entire podcast into seven languages, they said their goodbyes in their language of choice, or as they explained, "I'd like to say goodbye from my country."

In the podcasts, equity was also part of how the roles were defined—so that every child in Mrs. Felderman's class had a meaningful part. Podcasts became a meaningful way for the children to write—stories, jokes, acknowledgments, and goodbyes. Different segments in the podcasts allowed children to participate authentically and meaningfully, finding their place in this whole class project. As young children, the students in Mrs. Felderman's classroom were able to see themselves as capable of change, as able to foster a more just world—and to share their actions widely!

## REFLECTING ON TECHNOLOGY AS A TOOL FOR MEDIATING MULTICULTURAL TEACHING

Ask yourself: "What technology does my (pre)school have and how can this technology be used as a tool to mediate multicultural education beyond my classroom walls?" Technology can be a tool for breaking traditional barriers and engaging with the larger global community across time and space. Podcasting is an example of technology as a tool for mediating multicultural education, but there are multiple technological possibilities that lay ahead. This work is not dependent on a specific technological tool—it is about positioning the tool as a way for the class to consider multiple perspectives and points of view, to co-construct discussions that may not be present within the walls of any one classroom. It is about engaging in real communication. When Mrs. Felderman's 2nd-graders said, "We did it and so can you," they were really speaking to an audience throughout the world—and those geographic locations indicated in the ClustrMaps really came to life to them—expanding their learning possibilities. Are you ready to use technology as a tool to mediate your teaching? Think of it as a wonderful challenge and a worthy learning adventure—just as Mrs. Felderman did!

## FURTHER RESOURCES

Bers, M. U. (2008). *Blocks to robots: Learning with technology in the early childhood classroom*. New York: Teachers College Press.

Marsh, J. (Ed.). (2005). *Popular culture, new media and digital literacy in early childhood*. Abingdon, UK and New York: RoutledgeFalmer.

Vasquez, V. (2010). *Getting beyond I like the book: Creating spaces for critical literacy across the curriculum* (2nd ed.). Newark, DE: International Reading Association.

Vasquez V., & Felderman, C. B. (2012). *Technology and critical literacy in early childhood*. New York: Routledge.

# CHAPTER 8

# Storytelling and Story Acting: Creating Spaces for Children to Negotiate Change

Guess what? Guess what?! As young children interact with adults and with each other, they tell stories. "Amazingly, children are born knowing how to put every thought and feeling into story form" (Paley, 1990, p. 4). Storytelling is a common way in which we human beings make sense of our lives. Listening to the stories young children tell is an important way to start engaging in multicultural education. After all, multicultural education values firsthand knowledge and recognizes the importance of starting with personal, situated knowledge. This is done not by trying to workshop children's stories, getting them to fit them into beginning-middle-end sequences, but by truly listening to and learning from them. So, when a child says, "Guess what?!" it is important to take the time to listen and learn, allocating time and making space for stories in the early childhood classroom.

## WHY STORYTELLING AND STORY ACTING AS STRATEGIES FOR TEACHING MULTICULTURALLY?

Stories matter. Yet, traditionally in American schools, children's books tend to privilege Eurocentric stories. And print and books tend to be privileged over oral storytelling, even though oral storytelling traditions are well known and the practices of orally telling stories are very important in a variety of homes and cultures (Heath, 1983). In seeking to move away from Eurocentric stories as well as Eurocentric conceptions of what counts as literacy and learning, it is important to listen to the voices of children and the stories they tell—especially since such Eurocentric stories are often not representative of the experiences and lives of many children in today's early childhood classrooms. So, through the intentional inclusion of storytelling and story acting in the early childhood classroom (in contrast to reading and writing as traditionally defined), we teachers are transforming curriculum and teaching, making it more culturally responsive, inclusive, and multicultural.

In addition, by moving beyond often-privileged Eurocentric stories, we promote the recognition of self as cultural being and move toward the transformation of self, integral to critical multicultural education. We can question and redefine what the norm(al) is in classrooms and (pre)schools.

But to listen to children, we must recognize that while we think of ourselves as open-minded and tolerant, the ways in which we see the world are colored by the ways that we were raised, the experiences we had, and who we are. So, before listening to stories, it is important to recognize the filters we employ in listening—to recognize ourselves as cultural beings and consider the privileges afforded by our cultural locations and identities, as explained in Chapter 2. For example, Whiteness, heterosexuality, and Christianity all afford privileges in the United States and can serve as filters to listening.

Story acting is multicultural "because performance itself is grounded in action, reflexivity, and dialogue, a critical performative pedagogy denies students the comfort of a quiet, object position" (Louis, 2005, p. 344). In story acting, the teacher's role is that of a facilitator or "difficultator" and includes generating participation and recognizing multiple complexities, stimulating reluctant groups, working with communities, and knowing how and when to conclude an activity (Boal, 1995).

The challenging work in critical multicultural education is to find ways to engage in teaching that allows students to become subjects of their own learning—learning which may unsettle previously held thoughts, values, and belief systems. Story acting can get us started as it adds culturally situated and relevant stories to the traditional canon present in (pre)schools, expands the definition of what counts as worthwhile (from reading books to telling stories, from writing to story acting), values the voices and stories of students, and blurs the roles of teacher and learner. In doing so, story acting invites teachers to transform themselves (recognizing how they are cultural beings who see the world through cultural filters), the curriculum (adding stories and firsthand knowledge), and their teaching (blurring roles of teacher and learner).

## WAYS TO USE STORYTELLING AND STORY ACTING

"A day without storytelling is, for me, a disconnected day" (Paley, 1990, p. 3). Storytelling is a way in which young children make sense of their lives—whether or not the stories are "real." Storytelling and story acting can come to life in a variety of ways in the early childhood classroom. Vivian Paley (1990) embraced an entire curriculum based on storytelling and story acting. In play, the young children in Paley's preschool classroom told stories, which she recorded. Paley then transcribed these stories and referred to them in future interactions with the children in her classroom, thus valuing their voices and experiences, engaging in culturally responsive teaching. These children-authored stories were also acted out by the children on the classroom stage.

In Henry Padrón Morales's kindergarten classroom in Rochester, New York, stories are told and acted out. But instead of acting out the stories as they are told, Mr. Padrón seeks to illuminate some of the nuances regarding the characters in these stories. He invites children to act out stories that represent recurring oppressions, shaping interactions in the classroom, and considering power in relationships. He invites students to pay close attention to their "ideological bodies"—the relationship between physical bodies and the cultural associations of language, race, class, gender, sexual orientation, able-bodiedness, etc. that are imprinted on the human form (Pineau, 2002)—as a medium for experiential learning.

Through a performative approach, Mr. Padrón proposes that early childhood education can become a context not only for thinking about change but also for rehearsing and embodying change. He knows that distinct techniques of process are needed for individuals to transform the ways they relate to others in a diverse and more humane world. He invites his 4- to 6-year-old students to engage in such techniques, creating heightened awareness of the need for equity in the ways students treat each other and more fairness in terms of how the classroom community operates.

## GETTING STARTED

### Create a Safe Space

To get started, it is important to create a safe space for children to engage in play and to co-construct stories. While these spaces can be what characterize the classroom (where play is valued and seen as the main determinant of the classroom), in many early childhood classrooms, such spaces are hard to find—even being absent altogether. In such classrooms, it is important to create these spaces, finding wiggle room for play within the curriculum (Siegel & Lukas, 2008) so that we can pay attention to the stories children tell and co-tell.

While some teachers will find it helpful to write down children's stories and act them out, others, such as Henry Padrón Morales, find it helpful to move beyond listening to recording and enacting children's stories. Like Mr. Padrón, teachers may thus look across children's stories to identify generative themes that permeate the stories told by children in the class—such as intelligence being linked to race or gendered perceptions of play and dress. Then, the teacher may find a book or tell a story that encapsulates the basic premises associated with the generative theme, as described in Chapter 5. For example, Mr. Padrón used *The Black Frog* (Woods, 1999)—the story of an imaginary kingdom of frogs where "The Black Frog" struggles for acceptance in a world that privileges green frogs—as he sought to challenge children's perceptions of differences as deficits, specifically with regard to race, physical features, and dis/ability.

## Designate a Stage Using a Children's Circle

In addition, it may be helpful to designate a stage space in your classroom. This space can be demarcated by a rug or tape on the floor of the classroom. Children are then invited to sit around the outside while the acting goes on inside—on the stage. Paley (1990) described: "The stage in which we act out our stories is . . . sacrosanct when stories are performed" (p. 37). If your classroom is not big enough to demarcate such a space, you can push the furniture aside (against the walls of the classroom) and make a circle by asking the children to hold hands and expand their arms as far out as they can and then sit down. The circle of children will then serve as the demarcation of the stage. Or, find a space outside the classroom, such as the school's gym or cafeteria during off-hours.

Starting with a circle is very important. A circle is a democratic space where power hierarchies are (at least temporarily) broken (Freire, 1970). By recognizing the importance of making a circle and inviting children to participate each morning, Mr. Padrón brings the children together with a song, *Vamos hacer el círculo*, an invitation for all of the children to join in and circle around. He starts and ends each story acting and theatre session with a circle—a representation of the power of communities.

## Pay Attention to Body Awareness

With regard to body awareness—in moving toward story acting and theatre—it is important to help children become aware of their bodies as media for communication. In storytelling, too much emphasis is often placed on the ability to speak (in a certain language). Yet doing so may result in exclusionary practices—for example, the exclusion of Spanish, Mandarin, or Bengali, or the marginalization of African American Language. To foster more inclusive practices, teachers can listen carefully to the stories children tell while also paying careful attention to the embodied narratives negotiated in play. After all, children author stories before they can ever narrate their actions. So, honoring the body as a legitimate medium can contribute to making education more equitable and inclusive.

One of the ways of getting started is to invite children to performatively move away from their individualism toward a collective. A group exercise may help children start building on the notion of ensemble. Quite often children do things as individuals (as exemplified by side-by-side play in the earliest years) and don't see a connection between what they are doing and their classmates' interests and activities. Thus, there is a need for children to recognize that while many of their experiences are individual, many are also collective—thus making visible the ways in which children are both different and similar.

An exercise for getting started can be engaging in a slow walk, embodying specific emotions called out by the teacher, and freezing in motion—increasing body awareness. The children can then get in touch with their bodies, with their space, by looking at and acknowledging each other—and realizing that even though they have the same prompts (e.g., "walk angrily," "walk happily"), they are reacting and communicating in particular and unique ways. They also have to pay attention to each other, so they avoid collisions, make close calls, etc. This exercise mirrors the interactional process in the classroom—where children are unique individuals within communities, thus needing to function in both spaces at once.

While in the beginning this exercise can be done as children walk around in a circle, it is important to position children so that they are eventually walking toward each other and watch how their bodies react differently to the emotion being called out by the teacher. To bring awareness of how mechanical their bodies and movements are, you can switch action and word associations—starting by asking them to walk with the word *walk* and stop with the word *stop*. Then, help them demechanize their bodies, by asking them to walk when you say *stop* and stop when you say *walk*, for example. (For a full description of theatre games, read Cahnmann-Taylor & Souto-Manning, 2010.) By becoming aware of their bodies, children can add new dimensions to their play. In addition to the foreseeable benefits of this game, Mr. Padrón proposes that it leads children to freeze their actions and interactions and assess the best action to take within a given context. The children start bringing these learnings into their everyday lives. Thus, literally and metaphorically, this is a powerful exercise that brings the concept of awareness to the forefront of children's actions.

## Introduce Theatre Slowly

Although Mr. Padrón fully believes in theatre as a way to teach multiculturally, he starts introducing theatre gradually. He does not engage in full-fledged theatre activities until January. Yet, between September and December, he works with the 4- and 5-year-old children in his kindergarten class to create spaces for storytelling and story acting in more traditional ways. In doing so, his students come to value each other's voices and stories. They come to regard each other as worthy authors. This supplements and enriches the curriculum in his classroom. In January, Mr. Padrón moves from listening to stories, telling stories, and acting stories, to theatre for change, to rehearsing change via Boalian Theatre (Boal, 1979). The key elements are that they (teacher and students) have to know, trust, and respect each other as unique, fully capable, and worthy members of the classroom community. Together, they engage in the theatre process and reflect on it, socially imagining and rehearsing hopeful possibilities for change.

## CONSIDERING OBSTACLES, EXPLORING POSSIBILITIES

There are many potential obstacles to storytelling and story acting as ways of teaching and learning in early childhood classrooms. But one of the first that may come to your mind, perhaps due to the prevalent view of theatre as belonging outside of the classroom and not comprising real learning, may be about teaching the curriculum and meeting the standards along with district and state mandates. In application, theatre games (Boal, 1992) truly allow children to follow directions and to understand abstract concepts in real, embodied, and tangible ways. For example, in Mr. Padrón's kindergarten, young children were walking as a group and then were invited into "freeze" play (similar to a game you may have played during your childhood years). Because emotions were part of the kindergarten curriculum, Mr. Padrón incorporated them into the walk and freeze activities. After all, the children were more skillful at showing these emotions in their faces and with their bodies than they were with words (oral or written). Mr. Padrón thus brought together the kindergarten curriculum and Boalian theatre methods, creating a new and empowering practice. As Mr. Padrón said: "If they are going to be able to read anything, they should be able to read their own selves first." Through this exercise, children get in touch with and come to know themselves, with how they are moving and feeling. And, as Mr. Padrón underlined, "They can then start reading their contexts and rewriting their stories."

In addressing obstacles of time and space for storytelling and story acting, it is important to reconceptualize what counts as learning. "There is a tendency to look upon the noisy, repetitive fantasies of children as non-educational, but . . . without them, the range of what we listen to and talk about is arbitrarily circumscribed by the adult point of view" (Paley, 1990, p. 39). In other words, unless we listen closely, we are talking to and with ourselves in ways that continue to create inequity—thereby privileging those students with backgrounds aligning with our own. Given that over three-fourths of all early childhood teachers are White, affluent, and speakers of Mainstream American English (Saluja, Early, & Clifford, 2002), if we as teachers don't listen to and learn from the children we teach, we are likely privileging children whose home lives mirror ours while relegating and seg-regating others (Cochran-Smith, 2004; Haddix, 2008).

In addition, the schedule of your classroom may pose an obstacle—especially if it involves other teachers. When children are being pulled out many times each day (for services such as ESOL [English to Speakers of Other Languages], early intervention, and special education), it may become hard to find the time to engage in storytelling, story acting, and theatre. One solution may be to invite the teachers who provide additional services to push in rather than pull out. You can make the case that pushing in will better support students—avoiding transfer issues and fostering participation in an authentic community of learners. Sometimes this works, sometimes it doesn't. Often schedules are fragmented and focus on meeting the components set up by law or district policy and unfortunately may not necessarily provide the best experiences for all children. If pushing in is not a possibility, perhaps advocating to administrators and enlisting the help of parents and other family memebers may be the next step—to change the schedule of intervention and support services being delivered. Fragmented schedules do not allow for this kind of work to take place and can be rather stressful for teachers who feel that they are continuously focusing on the clock rather than focusing on children (Genishi & Dyson, 2009). Yet, all you need to get started is a period of 15–20 minutes.

Storytelling and story acting have great potential in the early childhood classroom considering that "every kind of learning differs from child to child, but nowhere are the behaviors more strikingly original than in storytelling. Even as the children borrow one another's ideas, they preserve a style and symbolism as unique as their fingerprints" (Paley, 1990, p. 40). Storytelling and story acting foster a true appreciation for diversities as resources. As a teacher, I hope that through storytelling and story acting with children, you will come to believe in the following: "Whenever I think about the children's differences, my sense of the excitement of teaching mounts. Without the uniqueness of each child, teaching would be a dull, repetitive exercise" (p. 47).

While story acting may seem dry and even mechanistic at first and the theatre exercises can remain at a metaphoric level and not be immediately accessible to young children, it is important to reflect on and talk about the process. After all, an integral part of engaging in story acting is to debrief, making sense of the exercises and stories, making relevant connections to self, coming to learn from differences and diversities, thus rehearsing and reflecting on change.

## ENACTING STORYTELLING AND STORY ACTING IN AN EARLY CHILDHOOD SETTING

What does an early childhood classroom look like when a teacher uses storytelling and story acting as ways to foster multicultural education and create spaces for children to negotiate change? While there are many ways of using storytelling and story acting to create spaces for children to negotiate change, here I invite you to enter Henry Padrón Morales's kindergarten classroom, listen to his students, and learn about how storytelling and story acting have become very important parts of teaching for equity and social justice. In doing so, you will see how young children acted up and created a multicultural learning community. Let's begin by learning about the teacher and the school where he teaches.

## The Teacher

Henry Padrón Morales teaches a dual language kindergarten at Duffy School No. 12 in Rochester, New York. He is Latino of Puerto Rican descent and has been a teacher for 28 years. Teaching is his second career. His first career was that of a full-time community activist. Before he went into a teaching certification program, he was very frustrated in law school. He knew that his professors were intellectually and scholarly sound, "but they didn't have praxis." When an advisor asked him if he had considered becoming a teacher, he decided to change his career path to become an early childhood teacher. He believes that the early years are where there is most hope for change. He got certified at the bachelor's degree level and then got a master's degree in early childhood bilingual education.

In addition to being a kindergarten teacher, Henry is a poet and percussionist and brings these facets of his identity to his classroom and his teaching. He starts the school day playing drums and inviting children to convene at the meeting area. He believes that teachers must genuinely care for the children with whom they teach and learn, be culturally connected to the children in their classrooms, and see teaching as a true opportunity for learning. He proposes that cultural connections are not limited to sharing similar backgrounds, but to learning from the children and their families with genuine respect and true appreciation, coming to understand who they are as cultural beings, as unique and valuable human beings.

## The Classroom

Welcome to Henry Padrón Morales's kindergarten classroom at Duffy Elementary School No. 12. Mr. Padrón teaches in a public school that has about 750 students in grades K–6. The school's students are 60% African American, 25% Latino/a, 13% White, 1% Asian/Asian American, and 1% Native American. Duffy Elementary School has 58 full-time teachers, and its rate of free and/or reduced lunch is 80%. Mr. Padrón's classroom is colorful and bright, being located in a large space that houses four open classrooms—two kindergartens and two 1st grades. The classrooms are demarcated by bookshelves or dividers and are located on the second floor, close to the bathrooms and the school's library. Within those half walls, stories come to life as Mr. Padrón listens closely to his students' stories, tells his own stories, and invites the children to act out stories promoting change one rendition at a time through story acting and through theatre.

*Scene 1.* It is almost 10 a.m. on a winter Monday, and 19 kindergartners are paired up, pretending to be clay and sculptor. After asking for permission from the clay, sculptors start their work, bringing their images to life. After sculpting, sculptors engage in a museum walk. They look closely at the sculptures, "just like a museum—when we go to a museum we don't touch the art" one of them says. After the activity is over, their teacher, Mr. Padrón, asks the children to hold hands and make a circle.

After making a circle, the children sit and look at Mr. Padrón. They start talking about what they did.

> *Mr. Padrón:* How did you feel being the sculptor?
> *Kevin:* People were not looking at me, but what I made Martin into.
> *Rachel:* Like a statue. Not like real people.
> *Isabel:* And when people touched the sculpture, I was afraid because it could break.
> *Mr. Padrón:* And how do you think the clay felt?
> *Tyrone:* Ahmmm, like it didn't know what we were trying to do.
> *Serafina:* Like they weren't even alive.
> *Jo:* The clay didn't even have a voice.
> *Mr. Padrón:* How did you feel being the sculpture?
> *Jay:* I felt like I was a penguin waddling on ice.
> *Mr. Padrón:* Why?
> *Jay:* Because that's what Patricia made me into.
> *Mr. Padrón:* And how do you think the sculptor felt?
> *Javion:* Like he could do anything. And didn't even have to explain nothing.
> *Mr. Padrón:* Who felt more powerful?
> *Jo:* The sculptor, because I chose to make Rachel into a robot. I had the strength, imagination, and the muscle to make her into a robot. So, I had the power.
> *PJ:* But I was powerful and I was the clay. I was a T-Rex. But [the sculptor] gave me the power.

As we think about everyday schedules in and across early childhood classrooms, even though choice time or play may be part of the plans, theatre is rarely included. Yet, theatre provides a way for children to represent their ideas, make sense of their worlds, and rehearse change. It provides a place for children to acknowledge (and even challenge) power dynamics. Through theatre, they are not bound to letters, numbers, and words. They are freed by images. Through theatre, young children can come to explore issues of power and equity. They can negotiate agentive positions in the classroom.

After this clay and sculptor exercise, later in the day, one girl was sad while waiting to go to the bathroom. Another girl, who was sitting next to her waiting for a turn to go to the bathroom, asked her, "Can I touch your face?" The girl who was sad nodded. The girl who asked to touch her face said: "Pretend you are clay." As I watched, I saw one girl sculpt a smile onto the other's face. "What are you doing?" I asked. The answer was: "I am the sculptor, and I am making her happy." "Are you happy?" I asked. The girl who had been sad responded: "Yes. I am. She made me happy."

*Scene 2*. Mr. Padrón and his kindergartners are sitting in a circle, on the floor. He shows *The Black Frog* (Woods, 1999) to the children and the following dialogue ensues:

*Mr. Padrón:* Who can remember how the story started?
*Juan:* They would not let the Black Frog in.
*June:* Into their kingdom.
*PJ:* The frog asks from the magic grasshopper.
*Asia:* For a wish!
*Serafina:* Yea. And then . . .
*Jo:* He turned green.
*Antonio:* And when . . . when he turned green, his
    feet were bigger than the other frogs.
*Lupe:* And his head too. It was a big head. Bigger than the green frogs.
*Joseph:* And he had smaller eyes.
*Jo:* He still had a hard time playing with them even
    when he was green like the other frogs.
*Tyrone:* He wanted to look like he did in the
    beginning of the story again.
*Isabel:* And he wanted to be Black again.
*Mr. Padrón:* So, I want you to think about the times when
    you wish you looked like someone else. What do you
    wish you were? Just think—you don't have to share.

The children started thinking. Mr. Padrón continued:

Now, we are going to divide our class in two groups. One will go to one side and the other will go to the other side (pointing to the sides of the room). One of you will be the green frog and the other the black. Ready? You will come to the middle and communicate with each other by freezing. Okay, come to the middle and freeze.

Children voluntarily—two at a time, one from each side—walked to the middle and froze in a pose that expressed the way they were feeling. As they did so, each time, Mr. Padrón said: "Look at them. Look at their bodies. Look at their faces. Look at their eyes. What do they tell you? What do you see? How are they feeling? Did you ever feel this way? When? What did you do?" Each time, students were pensive and seemed to carefully consider the questions asked. Many nods followed the "Did you ever feel this way?" question, confirming that many of them had felt out of place, sad, indignant, or excluded. Mr. Padrón responded: "Okay—go back to your group!" As the children went to their respective sides, Mr. Padrón invited them to think about other times when they themselves felt like that (the same way as they froze when they were pretending to be a green frog and the Black Frog).

Later Mr. Padrón asked the children to share some of their stories of when they felt like one of the green frogs or like the Black Frog. After children shared their stories, Mr. Padrón indicated his plans to engage in Forum Theatre with them—that is, selecting stories that resonated with many of the children, breaking them into three scenes, and seeking to change the oppressive outcome through spect-acting (spectators becoming actors and offering alternative actions). Thus, they were moving toward not only recognizing racial prejudice and oppression, but rehearsing change performatively. (For a full description of Forum Theatre in the classroom, see Cahnmann-Taylor & Souto-Manning, 2010.)

## The Teacher's Perspective

Mr. Padrón posits that within the current culture of standards and evidence-based education, diversities are often glossed over, and teachers can spew information the entire time, the entire year, as though they were depositing it in students' brains by way of a banking system of education (Freire, 1970). In doing so, Mr. Padrón believes that teachers continue to create inequities in their own classrooms. The power of theatre work is that it turns this process around and asks children to give teachers their stories and their struggles. In listening to students' stories, teachers have to respect them, resisting the urge to edit and repackage their stories. "I have to keep myself in check," says Mr. Padrón. This creates a different dynamic, blurring the roles of teacher and learner and creating spaces for students to position themselves as fully capable of promoting change, of changing their worlds, one action, one interaction at a time.

Mr. Padrón recommends starting with theatre games—think of them as a way of building community and as introductions to read alouds, transitions, etc. So, when children get used to playing theatre games (Boal, 1992), they are more prone to fully engage their bodies and explore story acting and theatre. They start seeing that while they can conform, they can also transform. His approach is about empowering children, starting with bits and pieces—with fun games. Then he moves toward building interrelations through The Machine (collaboratively building a machine with bodies—a larger structure of which individuals are a part, yet the whole is more meaningful than the sum of its parts), Invisible Theatre (making statements about what is happening with body images without revealing the acting, and living the situation as a real situation), and Forum Theatre (working together to transform inter/actions) (Boal, 1979; Cahnmann-Taylor & Souto-Manning, 2010). Storytelling and story acting allow us to move beyond data walls, Response to Intervention (RTI), and other curricular mandates. Mr. Padrón proposes that these mandates do not need to determine what happens in your classroom.

Multicultural teaching is about honoring the humanity of every child, valuing every child for who she or he is, and paying attention to their stories, to the ways they make sense of their lives. Why not give it a try? If you have 15–20 minutes, you can get started. It is a matter of prioritizing—the children over the curriculum, the humanity of every child over the number of areas that are mandated in the curriculum. Yet, prioritizing this work does not mean that the academic demands of kindergarten will go unmet. Through story acting and theatre, children engage in problem-solving, they employ complicated language, they bring to life and come to understand abstract concepts, they author sophisticated stories which are enriched when they act them out. They grow as human beings and as learners in the process.

"Learn to listen and practice listening. As teachers, we are not prepared to do that—to step back and listen. We talk and talk. As a society, we breathe competition and not collaboration," says Mr. Padrón. Story acting is about coming together as a community—not to see who is better or faster, but to co-construct a rendition of a story and perhaps move toward change. It is about listening to the stories children tell—in play and authentic interactions. "The genesis of multicultural teaching should be the children's stories," proposes Mr. Padrón.

## REFLECTING ON STORYTELLING AND STORY ACTING AS STRATEGIES FOR TEACHING MULTICULTURALLY

Finding time, genuinely listening to the voices and stories of children, and suspending judgment, thus moving away from professing and from the banking system of education, are key to engaging in this kind of teaching. It is important not to underestimate the power and brilliance of young children. They truly know about and experience issues of power and oppression. We need to listen to what children say (Paley, 1986) and ask questions that relate to their interests and stories. If you don't have time to ask questions when a story emerges, write those "kernels" down and return to them later (as Paley did). Mostly, show respect for the children's words and how they make sense of their worlds and they will respect you in return—they will respect each other.

For new teachers getting started in this work, it is important to get involved in studying about it. Read about it and start acting out—and up! Position yourself as a learner. And then, find a little bit of time, start with games, and then add to your repertoire. Story act and engage children in spect-acting (crossing the finite role boundaries of spectator and actor). And finally, resist the urge to offer solutions—even if you believe the solution you provide would work. Storytelling and story acting are about helping children problematize what is and collectively act upon a possibility, a rendition that may result in a different action. Suspend your judgment, step back, and facilitate. Respect children's solutions and create space for them to negotiate change, to negotiate their identities as agents.

## FURTHER RESOURCES

Boal, A. (1979). *Theatre of the oppressed*. New York: Theatre Communications Group.

Boal, A. (1992). *Games for actors and non-actors*. London; New York: Routledge.

Cahnmann-Taylor, M., & Souto-Manning, M. (2010). *Teachers act up! Creating multicultural learning communities through theatre*. New York: Teachers College Press.

Duffy, P., & Vettraino, E. (Eds.). (2010). *Youth and the theatre of the oppressed*. New York: Palgrave Macmillan.

Lobman, C., & Lundquist, M. (2007). *Unscripted learning: Using improv activities across the K–8 curriculum*. New York: Teachers College Press.

Mixed Company Theatre. (2010). *Teacher resources*. http://mixedcompanytheatre. com/education/teacher-resources/

Paley, V. G. (1990). *The boy who would be a helicopter: The uses of storytelling in the classroom*. Cambridge, MA: Harvard University Press.

# CHAPTER 9

# Reflecting on the Possibilities of Teaching Multiculturally: What If? What Next?

Unless someone like you cares a whole awful lot, nothing is going to get better. It's not.

—Dr. Seuss, *The Lorax*

Now that you have read about a variety of approaches, strategies, and tools for teaching multiculturally, it is important to take the time to think about which would work best for you. It would be easier to dismiss the many examples provided, yet, I invite you to "care a whole awful lot" as Dr. Seuss proposed in *The Lorax* (1971). If you do, then you can use these approaches, tools, and strategies to transform the way you teach. Furthermore, you can change the way your students learn—and give everyone a positive schooling experience, which may lead to hope for a better future. After all, care requires a sense of history and commitment. Care leads us to question injustices—such as the very high number of children of color who have been failed by American schools. Caring involves having to do something about these injustices—problematizing them and fostering transformative learning spaces. It is easy to say that we love teaching. Yet, as Shirley Brice Heath (2012) underlined: "Never love more than you care." If you truly love teaching (or would love to be a teacher), then be sure to care—to question what is and to bring to life what could be, creating multicultural learning communities in your own setting (Nieto, 1999).

In this final chapter, I invite you to reflect on the multicultural approaches, tools, and strategies presented in this book and consider possibilities, thus addressing the question: Now what? I am aware that you may find that none of the strategies fully work for you—because of the setting in which you teach or because the children you teach are 3 or younger and you cannot see yourself engaging in this kind of work with such young children. Nevertheless, I invite you to approach teaching multiculturally by reinventing these strategies and tools in your own context—after all, each is context-dependent and not meant to be exported. In helping you think through ways of continuing or getting started, in this chapter, we will reflect on the multicultural tools and strategies presented, thus considering possibilities for engaging in multicultural teaching. Then, we will learn from a Head Start teacher in Athens, Georgia, Maria Helena Mendonça Buril (or Miss Helena as her Head Start students call her), about creating "wiggle room" within the constraints of an existing program (Siegel & Lukas, 2008). In listening to Miss Helena, we will pay particular attention to ways in which reframing existing resources (especially within more structured settings) may open up possibilities and lead to more inclusive and multicultural practices. Finally, I invite you to envision spaces of possibility, considering questions that will help you devise a plan to get started and create spaces for teaching multiculturally. Ready? Let's begin!

## NOW WHAT? CONSIDERING POSSIBILITIES

As you read this book, you considered interviews, inquiry, culture circles, community resources and home literacies, story acting and storytelling, as well as technology as tools, strategies, and aproaches to teaching multiculturally in the early childhood classroom. You entered preschool to 2nd-grade classrooms in public and private settings throughout the United States. As you did so, I hope that you felt inspired and excited to get started, to teach multiculturally. If you are like me (or like many of the teachers with whom I have worked over the years), you are now trying to decide which one of these many promising tools, strategies, and approaches you will implement first. But you may also be thinking that your classroom may not look like Ms. Cowhey's, Dana's, Mr. Padrón's, Mrs. Felderman's, or Ms. Baines's. And—it won't. Because even if you decide to do what they did—to employ the same tool or strategy, to engage in a similar approach, it will come to life differently in your specific setting. There is nothing wrong with that. "Wrong" would be for all classrooms to look the same as this would signal "a very puzzling contrast—really an awesome disconnect—between the breathtaking diversity of schoolchildren and the uniformity, homogenization, and regimentation of classroom practices, from pre-kindergarten onward" (Genishi & Dyson, 2009, p. 4). So—instead of conforming to any model presented here, I invite you to reinvent these ways of teaching, bringing them to life in equitable, meaningful, and authentic ways in your own classroom.

### Think About Your Approach

As you begin, here are some things to take into account. First, consider the context where you teach. That context may inform the way that you choose to get started. Here are a few questions that may help:

- What are the technology resources available to you?
- Is the curriculum where you teach open and play- or project-based? Or is the curriculum regimented or scripted?
- Do you teach in a neighborhood school? Do the children you teach come from one community or from a few related communities?

Obviously, if you do not have the technology needed, it is hard to start using technology as a tool. So, that may not be the easiest way to get started. If you live in a highly populated area, interviews may be easy. If you live in a sparsely populated area, unless you have Skype or other technology for communicating across space, interviews may be harder to organize. Yet, they are not impossible. So, while these questions are not all-encompassing, they can help you start thinking about the way to get started that makes most sense within your unique context.

Second, take your preferences into account. If you are intrigued by the concept of interviews and would love to implement them, even if you are in a sparsely populated area, it may be the best way for you to get started. All in all, there is not just one way of getting started. There is no formula. Just take the first step and remember that "we make the road by walking" (Horton & Freire, 1990, p. 1).

Mostly, engaging in critical multicultural education is about embracing a perspective common to all strategies, tools, and approaches explored in this book, a critical multicultural perspective—listening to children, learning from them and their families, and creating spaces for multiple perspectives and points of view to expand the curriculum. To do so, as a teacher, you have to position yourself as a learner, thus blurring the roles of teacher and learner in your classroom (Freire, 1970). Then you may expand the classroom to involve the families and communities of the children who are members of your classroom. This involves helping families see how paramount their contributions are to their children's lives while also making visible the many positive and amazing ways they already are (and have been) contributing to their children's learning and growth. It is about highlighting the positives and respecting differences. It is about learning without comparing or prejudging. While this approach can be challenging, it is necessary if we are to create more equitable and democratic classrooms.

## Take Small Steps

As you consider possibilities and seriously ask yourself "What if?" and "Now what?" with a commitment to change that comes with caring, it is important to think about taking small steps. Some of the important small steps taken by the teachers featured in this book include: home and community visits, listening to what children say, seizing issues of unfairness and differences as opportunities for learning, critically using children's books as tools, and expanding the curriculum by bringing in voices from family and community members. While I know that you may have been drawn to other aspects of the practices featured in this book, I briefly invite you to consider possibilities for taking one of the small but important steps outlined below.

*Home and community visits* are deemed very important by a number of teachers featured in this book. At the most basic level, they allow the teacher to meet students' families and to give them the message that she or he cares. This is not a time for the teacher to judge the family's home or tell the family members about the importance of bedtime reading. It is a time for the teacher to learn about the family, their cultural practices, and their home literacies. It is a time to learn from the family and to honor them. As you read in Chapters 3 and 4, 2nd-grade teacher Mary Cowhey learned about family members' talents, occupations, and interests during her home visits. Then, she invited family members to expand and deepen the classroom learning by coming to the classroom for interviews and to contribute to inquiries. First-grade teacher Janice Baines (see Chapter 6) learned about the families' practices, music preferences, and literacies, and brought them to her 1st-grade classroom, creating bridges for children who had home languages and literacy practices which were not aligned with the ones over-privileged in school ("Standard English," book reading). Ms. Baines reminded us how important it is to schedule the visits at a time and place preferred by the family—some families may not feel comfortable at first welcoming the teacher into their homes. Both Ms. Cowhey and Ms. Baines recommend conducting home and community visits right at the beginning of the school year and then at least one more time throughout the year. So—if your year is about to start or just got started, this is a great time to take this step! If not, you can start planning home visits for next year or start halfway through the year. The choice is yours! I hope you will choose to take this important first step, thus better understanding where the children you teach come from and being able to build bridges between their home and school experiences and practices.

*Listening to what children say* is an important step taken by each and every teacher featured in this book. Mary Cowhey (see Chapter 3) listened to and recorded children's big questions, which in turn started interviews and inquiries in her 2nd-grade classroom. She wrote what students said on chart paper by the classroom meeting area—exactly as students said it. Dana Frantz Bentley (see Chapter 5) listened to what children said as they were interacting with each other and brought their questions to the center of culture circles—helping them problematize their assumptions regarding gendered colors and dress and many more things throughout the year. She wrote what her preschoolers said and sent their questions by email to their parents as a way of communicating about the learning that was going on in her preschool classroom. Janice Baines listened to the children and to their families, learning about the songs they liked, the cultural practices they shared, bringing them to the center of her teaching—with "I Can Read

Swag," for example. She kept a journal that helped her document and reflect on her learnings. Carol Branigan Felderman (see Chapter 7) took her students' questions seriously as they asked why the 2nd-graders at Bailey's Elementary School would not be able to go to the Baltimore Aquarium and clarified how the elimination of the trip was an issue of access and fairness. She listened to them as she helped them write down their questions to compose an invitation letter to their principal. She paid close attention to their concerns as she helped them prepare to meet with the principal and offered support as they worked on their podcast scripts. Finally, kindergarten teacher Henry Padrón Morales (see Chapter 8) listened to children's stories, recording them and creating the space for the children to act them out. He not only listened, but also found a book that represented issues of prejudice and power pertinent to his kindergartners—*The Black Frog* (Woods, 1999). *The Black Frog* then became the center of storytelling and story acting in his kindergarten classroom. So, in listening to the children you teach, it is important to pay close attention to what they say and how they say it. It is important to record what they say, bringing their stories, concerns, and questions to the center of the teaching and learning that goes on in your classroom. In doing so, you will find the children you teach to be motivated and engaged—truly invested in their learning. Ready to try? In doing so, you can start a new approach, strategy, or tool at any time of the year!

*Seizing issues of unfairness and differences as opportunities for learning* is central to the habits of each of the teachers featured in this book. These issues emerged from the children's concerns—they were not planned ahead of time or imposed by the teachers. They were critical to the children in each of these classrooms—and not necessarily to the teachers. A clear example of this is the issue brought up by Mrs. Felderman's 2nd-graders (see Chapter 7) and by Dana's preschoolers (see Chapter 5). So, in listening to what children say, paying close attention to their concerns, teachers can seize issues of unfairness and differences as wonderful opportunities for learning. Each of these teachers embraced such issues and positioned them at the center of their teaching, seeing conflicts as great opportunities to consider a variety of perspectives and points of view, thus fashioning a more inclusive and multicultural curriculum.

*Critically using children's books as tools* can be a promising way of raising children's awareness of issues, or as Dana Frantz Bentley articulated, of "lifting" their concerns. Children's books can provide a connection between children's immediate concerns and the larger societal phenomenon of gendered colors and dress, for example. In addition to seeing children's books being used in Bentley's preschool classroom (which included but were not limited to *My Princess Boy* [Kilodavis, 2010] and *And Tango Makes Three*

[Richardson & Parnell, 2005]), you read how Mary Cowhey (see Chapter 4) used children's books which may not be immediately considered multicultural, such as *Swimmy* (Lioni, 1963), *Farmer Duck* (Waddell & Oxenbury, 1991), and *Click, Clack, Moo: Cows That Type* (Cronin, 2000). She used the opportunity to lift the issue of where the children's clothes were made to a larger societal level—of working conditions and protests such as strikes. In both of these cases, children's books served as tools to raise awareness of the children's identified instances of unfairness as situated representations of larger phenomena, thus helping children see and understand more systemic injustices. Finally, in Janice Baines's classroom (see Chapter 6), she invited children to rewrite common Eurocentric stories such as *Goldilocks* in more culturally relevant ways, collectively authoring *Star Braid*.

*Expanding the curriculum by bringing in voices from family and community members* is also a powerful practice that addresses the Eurocentric nature of today's curriculum and teaching, of what is honored in (pre)schools in name of standardization, fidelity, and homogenization. Interviews are one obvious step for expanding the curriculum by bringing in the voices, perspectives, and points of view of family and community members. Interviews can serve as a stand-alone strategy—as portrayed in Chapter 3—or as a tool to be incorporated in approaches such as inquiry (see Chapter 4) or community resources and home literacies (see Chapter 6). Yet, interviews are not the only way to expand the curriculum by bringing in family and community voices. Storytelling is another (see Chapter 8) one of the possible ways of honoring the voices of families and community members—creating spaces to honor not only their voices and perspectives, but their ways of speaking. And so are home and community visits, which can generate a great amount of relevant information to the teaching of young children in more culturally responsive and multicultural ways. What are the ways in which you plan to make this happen?

Yet, all in all, the most important step is to come to *see the children you teach and their families as wonderful human beings with histories and practices that must be valued in classrooms and (pre)schools.* As a teacher, you can do your part by being sure that you know the children you teach as unique and worthy human beings with rich histories, which need to be an integral part of the curriculum they experience in school. Critical multicultural teachers care about each and every child—and commit to learning with them and from them. Can you take one of these small but important steps? Today? Tomorrow? If so—go ahead! Or is your teaching environment too structured? If you cannot yet see how you can get started, hopefully Maria Helena Mendonça Buril's approach can help you envision ways to create some "wiggle room."

## CREATING "WIGGLE ROOM": FROM A TEACHER'S PERSPECTIVE

From Miss Helena's perspective, creating "wiggle room" is about reframing existing resources. The more structured your teaching environment, the more creative you will have to be to truly honor the brilliance of each child. Below, I explain some of the ways in which Miss Helena reframed certain aspects of her practice, which I hope can serve as a starting point for you to reframe existing resources in your classroom and (pre)school, coming to situate them in more inclusive and multicultural ways.

### The Teacher

Maria Helena Mendonça Buril is a Latina lead teacher of a Head Start program in Athens, Georgia—in a class of seventeen 3- and 4-year-olds. Prior to working in Head Start, she was an Early Head Start teacher working with children 0–3 and their families in home and center settings. Miss Helena grew up in Recife, Brazil, where she went to normal school and became a teacher. As a child, Miss Helena went to a Freirean school, Instituto Capibaribe (the same school in which I was a student for 10 years). As an early childhood teacher, she also taught at this school until she immigrated to the United States. Upon immigrating, after a brief period when she saw her heavy accent as a barrier to teaching young children, she started volunteering in childcare at a local church. She became a home-based Early Head Start teacher in Georgia working with families and young children ages 0–3 in home settings. After a few years, she transitioned to a center-based Early Head Start. Since 2009, she has been a Head Start teacher working with children ages 3–5. In each of these settings, Miss Helena had to create wiggle room to engage in critical multicultural teaching. She recounts employing many of the practices enacted at Instituto Capibaribe in her teaching every day. Miss Helena's philosophy is that each child is a historical being, and unless you learn and understand his or her history, you are not really able to teach him or her in authentic and meaningful ways.

### Reframing Home Visits

Miss Helena does not believe that learning comes in a box that must be purchased. Ready-curriculum is ready for no one. Miss Helena believes that learning takes place in homes and communities, through participation and authentic interactions. With regard to parents and families, Miss Helena states: "It's about helping them see that they can use what they already have and that they are already doing it. So, it's really about helping them build on what they are already doing . . . helping them so that they can explain to others how they are already supporting their children's learning. It's about care and love . . . they respect me and know that I really care about their child." Miss Helena values the families with whom she has worked for who they are, for their rich histories, for what they *have*. Miss Helena recounts that she would tell family members: "You know what? You are already doing a lot here. Let me show you." And then she proceeded to show the family member all the ways in which he or she was already supporting the child in many areas, such as language, motor, and socio-emotional development. In doing so, she was able to draw on the strengths of families, showing family members the many resources already present in their homes that fostered learning and supported their child's growth—even when these resources looked different from those present in classrooms and (pre)schools.

## Reframing Teacher-Student Relationships

Miss Helena believes that in order to teach young children, you have to care—to truly care. And to care means to learn from and with each child, to form authentic relationships with the child and with his or her family, coming to see him or her for all the wonderful things she or he brings to the classroom. Miss Helena sees children as storytellers who can invite us into their worlds. She believes that as teachers . . .

> It is our responsibility to listen, but also to share who we are. We are all cultural beings. We are all historical beings. And we are not cultural and historical in the same ways. So, we need to learn from each other. As teachers, we need to learn about the children we teach—we need to listen to them and learn from their families.

Miss Helena reminds us to reframe undesired behaviors displayed by young children as a sign that more meaningful relationships need to be formed, that a more efficient way of communicating needs to be in place, and that a respectful and inclusive community of learners has not yet been fostered.

> It is not about fixing the child who is misbehaving. It is about me, as a teacher, seeing what I can do to change, how I can show him that I care and how I can show him that he is an important and valued member of the classroom community. . . . We must find a thread, something they like, as the lead, as the start of turning things around, of getting them involved, of showing them that we care. . . . It's a constant challenge, but a welcome one.

As a teacher, it is important to listen and learn about what lights up each child, what motivates the child, creating connections between their home and school worlds, between social and academic learning. In addition,

Miss Helena says that she tries to say yes as much as possible. When they ask, "Miss Helena, can I do this?" her default response is "Yes, you can." She wants them to see themselves as capable and in a positive light. So, unless there is a problem with their request, in which case she explains why their request cannot be granted, she says yes, as "this is their classroom too," she explains. She leaves all materials available and accessible for the children to use—not locking cabinets, but giving children access to any materials they desire. In addition to creating a more positive classroom environment, Miss Helena highlights that these practices foster independence and self-confidence in the children she teaches. While this requires a bit of patience to start, it is a necessary step that gives children the messages "Yes, you can" and "We believe in you." After all, letting the children get materials and put them away, creating their own play scenarios, takes longer than doing it yourself. Miss Helena emphasizes, "We need to allow children to have time to explore and learn and not time them." Then, when they have choice, independence, and time within a caring and positive classroom environment, they feel empowered and start doing things themselves—they take charge of the classroom. To begin, ask yourself:

- Am I giving the children I teach options and choices?
- Am I giving them a variety of opportunities to learn?
- Am I making a variety of materials available?
- Are the available materials meeting their needs and allowing them to communicate and engage in authentic and meaningful learning?
- Have I asked them what they want to do today? If so, have I honored their answers?
- Have I showed them that I genuinely care about them and believe in them? How?

These questions can help you start reframing (or continue to reframe) your relationships with the children you teach and form authentic relationships with them so that you can build on their strengths and invite children to come to see each other in a more positive light, creating a caring community.

## Reframing Mealtime

Often, part of a child's day in (pre)school is mealtime. In Miss Helena's classroom, these times are reframed as social times when children speak with each other and eat together. Miss Helena does not see this as a punitive time when children need to eat without speaking, but a time when children recount their learning adventures and share their thoughts with others. During mealtime, the children serve themselves and learn to push their chairs in after the meal, scrape their plates and pile them up so that they can be washed. They get used to the routine, but also to having mealtime as a social time, as a time for learning. In many schools, mealtime is not seen as an authentic learning time in the early childhood classroom. Yet, for Miss Helena, mealtime is a very important time as it happens both in the classroom and in the children's homes. It is not a time to judge the way that mealtimes happen in children's homes, but a time to sit and talk, to get to know each other better and to connect. Each day they thank the helpers for serving the food. They value each other's company as they come together for a meal. After all, isn't that what friends do when they get together for a meal? Why should it be different in the early childhood classroom?

## Reframing Centers

Center time! A time when the teacher typically envisions artificial space divisions between materials that are to be used a certain way by a predetermined number of children, right? Not in Miss Helena's classroom. Recognizing that children need more time to play and authentic spaces to explore their creativity, Miss Helena reframes her hour-long center time into a time when the children in her classroom can use any and all materials from any center (such as blocks, sensory table, art, puppets, manipulatives, housekeeping, library, science). Children create their own activities with as many or as few playmates as they'd like. There are no worries about how many children can participate in each activity or center—children negotiate participation in activities and learn how to get along without the teacher having to manage or dictate numbers. The children then bring together what may be seen as exclusive materials and activities, for example, housekeeping and block materials come together and they build a picnic. This is the time when they authentically interact with each other, develop oral language, author and enact stories, and foster friendships. And when they are done, children know where the materials go—and they put them back.

The space where a certain material started only signals where that material will return, but not what, how, by whom, and where it will be used. These are considerations that are—from Miss Helena's perspective—up to children's creativity and imagination. Miss Helena says: "I love when things can be used in different ways—how they come up with incredible ways to use materials I thought I knew about. They are so creative!" For Miss Helena, centers are places where related materials are stored, but the ways the materials are used and brought together are up to the children as they play. In her classroom, you can see Elias picking up a magnifying glass from the so-called science center and bringing it to the housekeeping area to investigate household items. Soon, Elias decides that the magnifying glass can also serve as a baby toy and as a lens for reading.

In Miss Helena's classroom, children are encouraged to re-create the meaning of objects through play. Denise lines up the puppets on top of the blocks to listen to a story from the so-called library center. Many storylines come to life as children are free to play without pressure as their teacher engages in flexibly reframing existing curricular structures in more child-centered ways. Miss Helena's role during this time is primarily to listen to what the children say and how they play—to observe, learn from, respond to, and grow with the children she teaches.

## Reframing Read Alouds

In addition to reading books that are representative of a variety of cultural and linguistic practices, Miss Helena makes time for storytelling during her designated read aloud times. She tells stories that invite children to see the positives in themselves and in each other. At times, she tells stories that her own son likes. Other times, she features children in her class as main characters, narrating what she observed. So, instead of overprivileging books, Miss Helena reframes read aloud times as collective story time.

There are two story times in her daily schedule. During each story time, Miss Helena tells stories as ways of connecting with the children. She listens to the stories students tell in the classroom during their play and refers back to them or retells them during storytime. At times, she takes note of what is happening and then narrates her notes as a play featuring class members as the cast. The children who are featured in the story recognize themselves in the narratives and offer additional details, co-authoring and co-telling the story. She is both a teacher and a learner—and she has to be comfortable not knowing exactly what is going to happen as many of the stories she tells are co-authored during play by the children she teaches. This allows them to become socialized in oral storytelling. During these stories, Miss Helena highlights the ways in which she and the children in her classroom speak differently. These practices allow every child to be framed as a capable author, a capable storyteller in the classroom. Further, such a stance invites the children to see their family practices as belonging in the classroom. Finally, by highlighting similarities and differences in her own classroom, Miss Helena creates spaces for stories that have not been published in books to be told in the classroom legitimately. In doing so, she inspires students to admire and respect the diversity of stories, voices, languages, and accents present in their classroom, (pre)school, homes, and communities.

## Reframing the Classroom Environment and Schedule

Miss Helena reframes her schedule to allow for as much play as possible—reframing existing curricular structures to make room for children to engage in authentic and child-directed play. She adopts a flexible curriculum. In her classroom, there are at least 2 hours of play daily—1 hour inside and 1 hour outside. She is not in a hurry to end these times, but extends them as much as possible as she sees play as the core of her classroom and the cornerstone of early childhood. "Making time for play is really important. You see the children playing in the private preschools. Why not in Head Start? Don't we want equal education? Then we must start with play." She critically considers curriculum mandates and makes decisions that primarily honor the children she teaches.

Miss Helena starts reframing the classroom environment by bringing in items from her home and inviting children to bring items from their homes (food packaging for the housekeeping area, for example) as well as photos of persons, places, and objects that are meaningful to them. She makes the classroom look like each of them, honoring the familiar and familial. In addition, Miss Helena makes sure that she has toys, books, and materials that represent a variety of cultures, languages, and experiences in her classroom. She has books that are written in English and in Spanish as well as in different Englishes (Southern English, African American English). Her classroom has books that feature a variety of races, cultures, families, and experiences. She says: "I am always looking for more materials that value and validate the cultures of the children I teach. I also want them to learn about the diverse world where they live." In reading these books, she talks with the children about how people speak differently—how their voices and their ways of speaking are unique. She uses her own accent as an example—thus approaching an important topic in a very open and personal way.

Miss Helena invites us to carefully consider how we convey messages through the ways we set up our classrooms and asks, "What stories do the walls and materials in your classroom tell?" If we only play European lullabies in an infant classroom, what message are we giving children? Who are the people featured on your walls? What do your posters and signs look like? What languages are present—audibly and visibly? These are important questions as we seek to reframe the environment in more multicultural and inclusive ways.

Through reframing existing and commonplace practices—those exemplified here and those that will be taking place in your own classroom and (pre) school—the "hope is that through educators' persistent, child-worthy efforts in classrooms and the larger public arena, we can look toward a future where children and teachers can work and play with less pressure and greater flexibility, where we are able to find playgrounds full of children with names as diverse as their stories" (Genishi & Dyson, 2009, p. 145). Miss Helena says:

The children I teach know that I respect and value each of them. I learn from their play. I listen to their stories. It is not about saying "mine is better," it's about respecting each other. They know I would be very sad if they were not respectful and loving and caring with each other. We are a community that plays together, a community that cares. I care.

## DEVISING A PLAN TO GET STARTED

While I cannot offer a list or a step-by-step plan for you to get started teaching multiculturally—as it would not be relevant or responsive to your specific classroom and to the children you teach—here are some questions that you may want to consider as you start devising a plan and reframing existing resources:

- Do you engage in home visits? If so, how do you plan to reframe your home visits multiculturally? If not, when do you plan to start engaging in home visits? And how will you frame these visits multiculturally?
- How will you as a teacher reframe your relationships with the children you teach and with their families?
- Do you have a mealtime in your classroom or (pre)school? If so, how can you reframe it to honor children's family practices and cultural backgrounds? Can you make it a more humane time?
- Do you have centers in your classroom? If so, how do they currently work and how do you plan to reframe them in multicultural and inclusive ways? If not, what are other curricular structures that could be reframed in more multicultural and child-centered ways?
- Do you have read alouds in your classroom? Do you ever engage in storytelling in your classroom? Why not? What if you did? Or—have you ever thought of inviting family and community members to tell stories?
- How can you reframe traditional curricular structures in your classroom to make wiggle room for play?
- Look around your classroom walls and materials. Document what you see. Quantify the books you have featuring White characters, the books that you have featuring characters of color. Do this with classroom materials, posters, and toys. What story does your classroom tell? What message is conveyed? How can you convey a more inclusive story? What are some of the books and materials that would value the cultures of your students? What are some of the books and materials that would expose your students to the diversities present in the world in which they live?

As you carefully and critically consider each of the questions above and the invitations issued throughout this book, I invite you to start planning ways of enhancing your teaching and learning—making your classroom a more multicultural place, a more equitable and inclusive learning space.

## CREATING SPACES FOR TEACHING MULTICULTURALLY

It is not merely important to create spaces to teach multiculturally—it is imperative. And while creating spaces for teaching multiculturally may initially seem to add to the many things that you are already doing, I invite you to listen to Miss Helena, who makes the case that engaging in this kind of teaching is less stressful and more fulfilling for all involved. She said:

> I want to go back home and be happy with what I did. To do so, I have to see the positives each child brings to the classroom. It is about them—about teaching so that they build on their strengths, but it is also about me. If I focus on their negatives, I set up a negative classroom. Then, I am stressed. If I focus on their positives and am excited about what they bring to the classroom—about who they are, the stories they tell—then I set up a positive classroom. Then I look forward to coming back day after day because it is not stressful. It's truly exciting. . . . I learned that when the kids are happy, I am happy too.

I sincerely hope that you will create spaces for teaching multiculturally in your own setting—making your life more positive and less stressful, while providing equitable and inclusive learning opportunities for all children. As you do so, I hope that you will encounter the joy of teaching in a way that is positive and promising—moving from seeing teaching as a chore or a stressful endeavor to seeing it as a pleasure. And—I hope that you will connect with others, explore transformative possibilities, and share your practice. But remember that no one can make you engage in this kind of work. The momentum comes from within us—from who we are and want to be as individuals, as teachers, as learners, as citizens committed to fostering a better world. And fostering a better world starts with one child and one classroom community at a time. I invite you to find something to love in every child you teach—and to truly care about them, by listening to them, respecting their families, being committed to educating them and advocating on their behalf. My greatest hope is that you will engage in teaching that is critically multicultural; that honors the brilliance of each and every child along with their rich cultures and particular histories—that you will engage in transforming the world one learning journey and one child at a time.

# Children's Books

Ada, A. F. (2004). *I love Saturdays y domingos.* New York: Aladdin Paperbacks.

Beaumont, K. (2005). *I ain't gonna paint no more.* Orlando, FL: Harcourt.

Boelts, M. (2007). *Those shoes.* Somerville, MA: Candlewick Press.

Bouwkamp, J. (2006). *Hi, I'm Ben! . . . and I've got a secret!* Rochester Hills, MI: Band of Angels Press.

Browne, A. (1998). *Voices in the park.* New York: DK Publishing.

Bryan, A. (2007). *Let it shine: Three favorite spirituals.* New York: Atheneum Books for Young Readers.

Bunting, E. (1991). *Fly away home.* New York: Clarion Books.

Bunting, E. (1994). *A day's work.* New York: Clarion Books.

Bunting, E. (2006). *One green apple.* New York: Clarion Books.

Campbell, N. (2005). *Shi-shi-etko.* Toronto, Canada: Groundwood Books/House of Anansi Press.

Choi, Y. (2003). *The name jar.* New York: Knopf Books.

Cohn, D. (2002). *¡Sí, se puede! / Yes, we can!: Janitor strike in L.A.* El Paso, TX: Cinco Puntos Press.

Colato Laínez, R. (2005). *I am René, the Boy/Soy René El Niño.* Houston, TX: Piñata Books.

Colato Laínez, R. (2009). *René has two last names/René tiene dos apellidos.* Houston, TX: Piñata Books.

Coleman, E. (1996). *White socks only.* Morton Grove, IL: Albert Whitman & Company.

Collier, B. (2000). *Uptown.* New York: Henry Holt and Co.

Cooper, M (1998). *Gettin' through Thursday.* New York: Lee & Low Books.

Cronin, D. (2000). *Click, clack, moo: Cows that type.* New York: Simon & Schuster Books for Young Readers.

DiSalvo-Ryan, D. (1997). *Uncle Willie and the soup kitchen.* New York: HarperCollins.

Foley, G. (2009). *Good luck bear.* New York: Viking.

Foley, G. (2009). *Willoughby and the lion.* New York: The Bowen Press.

Foley, G. (2011). *Purple little bird.* New York: HarperCollins, Balzer + Bray.

Giovanni, N. (2005). *Rosa.* New York: Square Fish.

González, R. (2005) *Antonio's card/La tarjeta de Antonio.* San Francisco: Children's Book Press.

Grimes, N. (1995). *C is for city.* New York: HarperCollins.

Gunning, M. (2004). *A shelter in our car.* San Francisco: Children's Book Press.

Heelan, J. (2000). *Rolling along: The story of Taylor and his wheelchair.* Atlanta, GA: Peachtree.

Herrera, J. F. (2000). *The upside down boy/El niño de cabeza.* San Francisco: Children's Book Press.

Herrera, J. P. (2003). *Super cilantro girl.* San Francisco: Children's Book Press.

Horowitz, D. (2007). *Five little gefiltes.* New York: G. P. Putnam's Sons.

Hru, D. (2002). *Tickle tickle.* Brookfield, CT: Roaring Book Press.

Hughes, L. (2009). *My people.* New York: Atheneum Books for Young Readers.

Jiménez, F. (1998) *La mariposa.* New York: Houghton Mifflin.

Kates, B. (1992). *We're different, we're the same, and we're all wonderful!* New York: Random House.

Keats, E. J. (1962). *The snowy day.* New York: Viking.

Keats, E. J. (1999). *Apt. 3.* New York: Viking and Puffin Books.

Kilodavis, C. (2010). *My princess boy.* New York: Aladdin.

Krull, K. (2003). *Harvesting hope: The story of Cesar Chavez.* Orlando, FL: Harcourt.

Lee, S., & Lewis Lee, T. (2006). *Please, baby, please.* New York: Simon & Schuster Books for Young Readers.

Lester, H. (1999). *Hooway for Wodney Wat.* New York: Walter Lorraine Books.

Levine, E. (2007). *Henry's freedom box.* New York: Scholastic Press.

Lioni, L. (1963). *Swimmy.* New York: Alfred A. Knopf, Inc.

Lobel, A. (1971). *Frog and toad together.* New York: HarperCollins Children's Books.

McBrier, P. (2001). *Beatrice's goat.* New York: Atheneum Books for Young Readers.

McCall, E. S. (1961). *How we get our clothing.* Chicago, IL: Benefic Press.

McKissack, P. C. (2001). *Goin' someplace special.* New York: Simon & Schuster Books for Young Readers.

Milway, K. S. (2008). *One hen: How one small loan made a big difference.* Tonawanda, NY: Kids Can Press Ltd.

Mochizuki, K. (1993). *Baseball saved us.* New York: Lee & Low Books.

Mora, P. (2009). *Book fiesta!: Celebrate children's day/book day/Celebremos el día de los niños/el día de los libros.* New York: HarperCollins Children's Books.

Morales, Y. (2003). *Just a minute: A trickster tale and counting book.* San Francisco: Chronicle Books.

Morales, Y. (2008). *Just in case: A trickster tale and Spanish alphabet book.* New York: Roaring Book Press.

Muth, J. (2000). *The three questions.* New York: Scholastic.

Muth, J. (2005). *Zen shorts.* New York: Scholastic.

Nelson, K. (2005). *He's got the whole world in his hands.* New York: Dial Books for Young Readers.

Peete, H. R. (2010). *My brother Charlie.* New York: Scholastic.

Perez, A. I. (2002). *My diary from here to there/Mi diario de aquí hasta allá.* New York: Lee & Low Books.

Rappaport, D., & Collier, B. (2001). *Martin's big words: The life of Dr. Martin Luther King, Jr.* New York: Hyperion Books for Children.

Recorvits, H. (2003). *My name is Yoon.* New York: Frances Foster Books.

Richardson, J., & Parnell, P. (2005). *And Tango makes three.* New York: Simon & Schuster Books for Young Readers.

Ringgold, F. (1991). *Tar beach.* New York: Crown.

Say, A. (2002). *Home of the brave.* New York: Walter Lorraine Books.

Seuss Geisel, T. (1971). *The lorax.* New York: Random House.

Shange, N., & Nelson, K. (2004). *Ellington was not a street.* New York: Simon & Schuster Books For Young Readers.

Smith, C. L. (2000). *Jingle dancer.* New York: Morrow Junior Books.

Soto, G. (1993). *Too many tamales.* New York: PaperStar Books.

Sockabasin, A. (2005). *Thanks to the animals.* Gardiner, ME: Tilbury House.

Tafolla, C. (2009). *What can you do with a paleta?/¿Qué puedes hacer con una paleta?* Berkeley, CA: Tricycle Press.

Uchida, Y. (1993). *The bracelet.* New York: PaperStar Books.

Waddell, M., & Oxenbury, H. (1991). *Farmer duck.* London, UK: Walker Books Ltd.

Waters, K., & Slovenz-Low, M. (1990). *Lion dancer: Ernie Wan's Chinese new year.* New York: Scholastic.

Wayland, A. (2009). *New year at the pier: A Rosh Hashanah story.* New York: Dial Books for Young Readers.

Weiss, G., & Thiel, B. (1967). *What a wonderful world.* New York: Atheneum Books for Young Readers.

Wiles, D. (2001). *Freedom summer.* New York: Aladdin Paperbacks.

Winter, J. (2009). *Nasreen's secret school: A true story from Afghanistan.* New York: Beach Lane Books.

Woods, E. (1999). *The black frog.* Montgomery, AL: Emmett L. Woods.

Wyeth, S. (1998). *Something beautiful.* New York: Dragonfly Books.

# References

Allen, J. (2007). *Creating welcoming schools: A practical guide to home-school part-nerships with diverse families.* New York: Teachers College Press.

Banks, J. (1993). Multicultural education for young children: Racial and ethnic at-titudes and their modification. In B. Spodek (Ed.), *Handbook of research on the education of young children* (pp. 236–250). New York: Macmillan.

Banks, J. (1994). Transforming the mainstream curriculum. *Educational Leader-ship, 51*(8), 4–8.

Banks, J. (1996). *Cultural diversity and education: Foundations, curriculum and teaching* (5th ed.). Boston: Allyn & Bacon.

Banks, J. (2004). Multicultural education: Historical development, dimensions, and practice. In J. A. Banks & C. A. Banks (Eds.), *Handbook of research on multi-cultural education* (2nd ed.) (pp. 3–29). San Francisco, CA: Jossey Bass.

Banks, J. (2007). Series foreword. In C. D. Lee, *Culture, literacy, and learning: Tak-ing bloom in the midst of the whirlwind* (pp. xi–xv). New York: Teachers Col-lege Press.

Banks, J., & Banks, C. A. M. (Eds.). (2004). *Multicultural education: Issues and perspectives* (5th ed.). Hoboken, NJ: John Wiley.

Bartolomé, L., & Macedo, D. (1997). Dancing with bigotry: The poisoning of racial and ethnic identities. *Harvard Educational Review, 67*(2), 222–244.

Bentley, D. F. (2011). "Rights are the words for being fair": Multicultural practice in the early childhood classroom. *Early Childhood Education Journal*, DOI: 10.1007/s10643-011-0492-7.

Bentley, D. F. (in press). *Everyday artists: Inquiry and creativity in the early child-hood classroom.* New York: Teachers College Press.

Bers, M. U. (2008). *Blocks to robots: Learning with technology in the early child-hood classroom.* New York: Teachers College Press.

Bishop, R. S. (2007). *Free within ourselves: The development of African American children's literature.* Portsmouth, NH: Heinemann.

Boal, A. (1979). *Theatre of the oppressed.* New York: Theatre Communications Group.

Boal, A. (1992). *Games for actors and non-actors.* London; New York: Routledge.

Boal, A. (1995). *Rainbow of desire: The Boal method of theatre and therapy poli-tics.* London: Routledge.

Bronson, P., & Merryman, A. (2009, September 5). Even babies discriminate. *News-week.* Retrieved from http://www.newsweek.com/2009/09/04/see-baby-discrim inate.html

Cahnmann-Taylor, M., & Souto-Manning, M. (2010). *Teachers act up! Creating multicultural learning communities through theatre.* New York: Teachers College Press.

Carter, R., & Goodwin, A. L. (1994). Racial identity and education. *Review of Research in Education, 20,* 291–336.

Cazden, C. (1986). Classroom discourse. In M. C. Wittrock (Ed.), *Handbook of research on teaching* (Vol. 3, pp. 432–463). New York: Macmillan.

Chang, B., & Au, W. (2008). You're Asian, how could you fail math?: Unmasking the myth of the model minority. *Rethinking Schools, 22*(2), 15–19.

Chilcott, L. (Producer), & Guggenheim, D. (Director). (2010). *Waiting for superman* [Motion picture]. United States: Paramount.

Cochran-Smith, M. (2004). *Walking the road: Race, diversity, and social justice in teacher education.* New York: Teachers College Press.

Cowhey, M. (2006). *Black ants and Buddhists: Thinking critically and teaching differently in the primary grades.* Portland, MN: Stenhouse.

Cowhey, M. (2009). "Where's your shirt from?" Second graders learn to use data to change the world. *Connect, 23*(2), 14–17.

De Gaetano, Y., Williams, L. R., & Volk, D. (1998). *Kaleidoscope: A multicultural approach for the primary classroom.* Upper Saddle River, NJ: Merrill Prentice Hall.

Delpit, L., & Dowdy, J. K. (Eds.). (2002). *The skin that we speak: Thoughts on language and culture in the classroom.* New York: The New Press.

Derman-Sparks, L., & Edwards, J. (2010). *Anti-bias education for young children and ourselves.* Washington, DC: National Association for the Education of Young Children.

Derman-Sparks, L., & Ramsey, P. (2011). *What if all the kids are white? Anti-bias multicultural education with young children and families* (2nd ed.). New York: Teachers College Press.

Dewey, J. (1938). *Experience and education.* New York: Collier Books.

Duffy, P., & Vettraino, E. (Eds.). (2010). *Youth and the theatre of the oppressed.* New York: Palgrave Macmillan.

Dyson, A. H., & Genishi, C. (2005). *On the case: Approaches to language and literacy research.* New York: Teachers College Press.

Education: Forced busing and white flight. (1978). *Time.* http://www.time.com/time/magazine/article/0,9171,912178-1,00.html

Fennimore, B. S. (2000). *Talk matters: Refocusing the language of public schooling.* New York: Teachers College Press.

Freire, P. (1970). *Pedagogy of the oppressed.* New York: Continuum.

Freire, P. (1973). *Education for critical consciousness.* New York: Seabury Press.

Freire, P. (1985). *The politics of education.* Westport, CT: Bergin & Garvin.

Freire, P. (1998). *Teachers as cultural workers: Letters to those who dare teach.* Boulder, CO: Westview Press.

Freire, P., & Macedo, D. (1987). *Literacy: Reading the word and the world.* Westport, CT: Bergin & Garvey.

Frey, W. H. (2011). *The new metro minority map: Regional shifts in Hispanics, Asians, and Blacks from census 2010*. Washington, DC: Brookings Institution.

Gay, G. (1994). *At the essence of learning: Multicultural education*. West Lafayette, IN: Kappa Delta Pi.

Genishi, C., & Dyson, A. H. (2009). *Children, language, and literacy: Diverse learners in diverse times*. New York: Teachers College Press.

Genishi, C., & Dyson, A. H. (2012). Racing to the top: Who's accounting for the children? *Bankstreet Occasional Papers*, 27. Retrieved from http://bankstreet.edu/occasional-papers/issues/occasional-papers-27/part-ii/whos-accounting-children/

Genishi, C., & Goodwin, A. L. (Eds.). (2008). *Diversities in early childhood education: Rethinking and doing*. New York: Routledge.

Giroux, H. (1985). Introduction. In P. Freire, *The politics of education: Culture, power, and liberation* (pp. xi–xxvi). Westport, CT: Bergin & Garvin.

Giroux, H. (1992). *Border crossings: Cultural workers and the politics of education*. New York: Routledge.

Gonzalez, N., Moll, L. C., & Amanti, C. (2005). *Funds of knowledge: Theorizing practices in households and classrooms*. Mahwah, NJ: Lawrence Erlbaum Associates.

Goodwin, A. L., Cheruvu, R., & Genishi, C. (2008). Responding to multiple diversities in early childhood education. In C. Genishi & A. L. Goodwin (Eds.), *Diversities in early childhood education: Rethinking and doing* (pp. 3–10). New York: Routledge.

Goodwin, A. L., & Genor, M. (2008). Disrupting the taken-for-granted: Autobiographical analysis in preservice teacher education. In C. Genishi & A. L. Goodwin (Eds.), *Diversities in early childhood education: Rethinking and doing* (pp. 201–218). New York: Routledge.

Gorski, P. (2010a). *Five shifts of consciousness for multicultural educators*. Retrieved from http://www.edchange.org/handouts/paradigmshifts.pdf/

Gorski, P. (2010b). *The challenge of defining multicultural education*. Retrieved from http://www.edchange.org/multicultural/

Grant, C. A. (2008). An essay on searching for curriculum and pedagogy for African American students: Highlighted remarks regarding the role of gender. *American Behavioral Scientist, 51*(7), 885–906.

Grant, C. A., & Sleeter, C. E. (1990). *After the school bell rings* (2nd ed.). Philadelphia, PA: Falmer.

Grant, C. A., & Sleeter, C. (2007). *Doing multicultural education for achievement and equity*. New York: Routledge.

Gregory, E., Long, S., & Volk, D. (Eds). (2004). *Many pathways to literacy: Young children learning with siblings, peers, grandparents, and communities*. London, UK: RoutledgeFalmer.

Haddix, M. (2008). Beyond sociolinguistics: Toward a critical approach to cultural and linguistic diversity in teacher education. *Language and Education, 22*(5), 254–270.

Heath, S. B. (1983). *Ways with words: Language, life, and work in communities and classrooms*. New York: Cambridge University Press.

Heath, S. B. (2012, May). *Four-lettered words: Caution and a bit of persuasion*. 2012 Teachers College Medalist Dinner, New York, NY.

Hoffman, D. M. (1996). Culture and self in multicultural education: Reflections on discourse, text, and practice. *American Educational Research Journal, 33*(3), 545–569.

Horton, M., & Freire, P. (1990). *We make the road by walking: Conversations on education and social change*. Philadelphia, PA: Temple University Press.

Israelsen-Hartley, S. (2010). *Acclaimed children's books have few characters with disabilities*. Retrieved from http://www.deseretnews.com/article/700096333/ Acclaimed-childrens-books-have-few-characters-with-disabilities. html?pg=all

Jennings, L., & Mills, H. (2009). Constructing a discourse of inquiry: Findings from a five-year ethnography at one elementary school. *Teachers College Record, 111*(7), 1583–1618.

Kagan, S. L., & Kauerz, K. (Eds.). (2012). *Early childhood systems: Transforming early learning*. New York: Teachers College Press.

Kagan, S. L., Kauerz, K., & Tarrant, K. (2008). *The early care and education teaching workforce at the fulcrum: An agenda for reform*. New York: Teachers College Press.

Kinloch, V. (2010). *Harlem on our minds: Place, race, and the literacies of urban youth*. New York: Teachers College Press.

Koplow, L. (2008). *Bears, bears everywhere! Supporting children's emotional health in the classroom*. New York: Teachers College Press.

Kozol, J. (1991). *Savage inequalities: Children in America's schools*. New York: Crown.

Ladson-Billings, G. (1994). *The dreamkeepers: Successful teachers of African American children*. San Francisco: Jossey-Bass Publishers.

Lee, E., Menkart, D., & Okazawa-Rey, M. (Eds.). (2002). *Beyond heroes and holidays: A practical guide to K–12 anti-racist, multicultural education and staff development* (2nd ed.). Washington, DC: Teaching for Change.

Lewis, C., Enciso, P., & Moje, E. (Eds.). (2007). *Reframing sociocultural research on literacy: Identity, agency, & power*. Mahwah, NJ: LEA.

Lindfors, J. (1999). *Children's inquiry: Using language to make sense of the world*. New York: Teachers College Press.

Lindfors, J. (2008). *Children's talk: Connecting reading, writing, and talk*. New York: Teachers College Press.

Lobman, C., & Lundquist, M. (2007). *Unscripted learning: Using improv activities across the K–8 curriculum*. New York: Teachers College Press.

Long, S. (2011). *Supporting students in a time of core standards: English language arts grades prek–2*. Urbana, IL: National Council of Teachers of English.

Louis, R. (2005). Performing English, performing bodies: A case for critical performative language pedagogy. *Text & Performance Quarterly, 25*(4), 334–353.

Macneil/Lehrer Productions. (2005). *Do you speak American? From sea to shining sea: English varieties, African American English.* http://www.pbs.org/speak/seatosea/americanvarieties/AAVE/

Mansell, W., & Curtis, P. (2009). *Segregation in schools fuelled by "white flight," report warns.* Retrieved from http://www.guardian.co.uk/education/2009/jul/10/segregation-race-schools#history-link-box

Marsh, J. (Ed.). (2005). *Popular culture, new media and digital literacy in early childhood.* Abingdon, UK and New York: RoutledgeFalmer.

McLaren, P. (1994). Multiculturalism and the postmodern critique: Towards a pedagogy of resistance and transformation. In H. A. Giroux & P. McLaren (Eds.), *Between borders: Pedagogy and the politics of cultural studies* (pp. 192–222). New York: Routledge.

Mills, H., & Donnelly, A. (Eds). (2001). *From the ground up: Creating a culture of inquiry.* Portsmouth, NH: Heinemann.

Mills, H., O'Keefe, T., & Jennings, L. (2004). *Looking closely and listening carefully: Learning literacy through inquiry.* Urbana, IL: National Council of Teachers of English.

Mills, H. T., O'Keefe, & Whitin, D. (1996). *Mathematics in the making: Authoring ideas in primary classrooms.* Portsmouth, NH: Heinemann.

Mixed Company Theatre. (2010). *Teacher resources.* http://mixedcompanytheatre.com/education/teacher-resources/

Moll, L., & Greenberg, J. (1990). Creating zones of possibilities: Combining social contexts for instruction. In L. Moll (Ed.), *Vygotsky and Education: Instructional implications and applications of sociohistorical psychology* (pp. 319–348). New York: Cambridge University Press.

Moll, L., Amanti, C., Neff, D., & González, N. (1992). Funds of knowledge for teaching: Using a qualitative approach to connect homes and classrooms. *Theory into Practice, 31,* 132–141.

Nieto, S. (1996). *Affirming diversity: The sociopolitical context of multicultural education* (2nd ed.). White Plains, NJ: Longman.

Nieto, S. (1999). *The light in their eyes: Creating multicultural learning communities.* New York: Teachers College Press.

Nieto, S. (2000). Placing equity front and center: Some thoughts on transforming teacher education for a new century. *Journal of Teacher Education, 51*(3), 180–187.

Nieto, S. (2002). *Language, culture, and teaching: Critical perspectives for a new century.* Mahwah, NJ: Lawrence Erlbaum Associates.

Nieto, S. (2003). *What keeps teachers going?* New York: Teachers College Press.

Nieto, S. (2010). *Language, culture, and teaching: Critical perspectives* (2nd ed.). New York: Routledge.

Nieto, S., & Bode, P. (2011). *Affirming diversity: The sociopolitical context of multicultural education* (6th ed.). White Plains, NJ: Longman.

Oakes, J., & Lipton, M. (1999). *Teaching to change the world*. Boston, MA: McGraw-Hill.

Oyler, C. (2011). *Actions speak louder than words: Community activism as curriculum*. New York: Routledge.

Paley, V. G. (1986). On listening to what the children say. *Harvard Educational Review, 56*(2), 122–131.

Paley, V. G. (1990). *The boy who would be a helicopter: The uses of storytelling in the classroom*. Cambridge, MA: Harvard University Press.

Palfrey, J., & Gasser, U. (2010). *Born digital: Understanding the first generation of digital natives*. New York: Basic Books.

Pineau, E. L. (2002). Critical performative pedagogy: Fleshing out the politics. In N. Stucky & C. Wimmer (Eds.), *Teaching performance studies* (pp. 41–54). Carbondale, IL: Southern Illinois University Press.

Purcell-Gates, V. (Ed.). (2007). *Cultural practices of literacy: Case studies of language, literacy, social practice, and power*. New York: Routledge.

Ramsey, P. (2004). *Teaching and learning in a diverse world* (3rd ed.). New York: Teachers College Press.

Ramsey, P. G., & Williams, L. (Eds). (2003). *Multicultural education: A sourcebook*. New York: Routledge.

Rickford, J. R., & Rickford, R. J. (2000). *Spoken soul: The story of Black English*. New York: Wiley.

Rogovin, P. (1998). *Classroom interviews: A world of learning*. Portsmouth, NH: Heinemann.

Saluja, G., Early, D. M., & Clifford, R. M. (2002). Demographic characteristics of early childhood teachers and structural elements of early care and education in the United States. *Early Childhood Research and Practice, 4*(1). Retrieved from http://ecrp.uiuc.edu/v4n1/saluja.html.

Shor, I. (1990). Liberation education: An interview with Ira Shor. *Language Arts, 67*(4), 342–353.

Siegel, M., & Lukas, S. (2008). Room to move: How kindergartners negotiate literacies and identities in a mandated balanced literacy curriculum. In C. Genishi & A. L. Goodwin (Eds.), *Diversities in early childhood: Rethinking and doing* (pp. 29–47). New York: Routledge.

Sleeter, C., & Bernal, D. D. (2003). Critical pedagogy, Critical race theory, and antiracist education: Implications for multicultural education. In J. Banks & C. M. Banks (Eds.), *Handbook of research on multicultural education* (2nd ed.). San Francisco: Jossey-Bass.

Smitherman, G. (2006). *Word from the mother: Language and African Americans*. New York: Routledge.

Souto-Manning, M. (2010a). Challenging ethnocentric literacy practices: (Re)Positioning home literacies in a Head Start classroom. *Research in the Teaching of English, 45*(2), 150–178.

Souto-Manning, M. (2010b). *Freire, teaching, and learning: Culture circles across contexts*. New York: Peter Lang.

Souto-Manning, M. (2010c). Teaching English learners: Building on cultural and linguistic strengths. *English Education, 42*(3), 249–263.

Steiner, S., Krank, H., McLaren, P., & Bahruth, R. (2000). *Freirean pedagogy, praxis, and possibilities: Projects for the new millennium*. New York: Falmer Press.

Valdés, G. (1996). *Con respeto: Bridging the distances between culturally diverse families and schools*. New York: Teachers College Press.

Vasquez, V. (2004). *Negotiating critical literacies with young children*. Mahwah, NJ: LEA.

Vasquez, V. (2010). *Getting beyond I like the book: Creating spaces for critical literacy across the curriculum* (2nd ed.). Newark, DE: IRA.

Vasquez V., & Felderman, C. B. (2012). *Technology and critical literacy in early childhood*. New York: Routledge.

Wells, D. (1995). Leading grand conversations. In N. Roser & M. Martinez (Eds.), *Book talk and beyond: Children and teachers respond to literature* (pp. 132–139). Newark, DE: IRA.

Wells, G. (1999). *Dialogic inquiry: Towards a sociocultural practice and theory of education*. Cambridge, UK: Cambridge University Press.

Whitehouse, M., & Colvin, C. (2001). "Reading" families: Deficit discourse and family literacy. *Theory into Practice, 40,* 212–219.

Zumwalt, K., & Craig, E. (2005). Teachers' characteristics: Research on the demographic profile. In M. Cochran-Smith & K. M. Zeichner (Eds.), *Studying teacher education: The report of the AERA panel on research and teacher education* (pp. 111–156). Mahwah, NJ: LEA.

# Index

# About the Author

**Mariana Souto-Manning** is Associate Professor of Education in the Department of Curriculum and Teaching at Teachers College, Columbia University. She is a former preschool and primary grades teacher and now teaches courses related to early literacy and multicultural education. She is author of *Freire, Teaching, and Learning: Culture Circles Across Contexts*, co-author of *Teachers Act Up!: Creating Multicultural Learning Communities Through Theatre*, and co-editor of *Sites of Possibility: Critical Dialogue Across Educational Settings*. From a critical perspective, her research examines the sociocultural and historical foundations of early schooling, language development, and literacy practices in pluralistic settings. She studies how children, families, and teachers from diverse backgrounds shape and are shaped by discursive practices. Her work can be found in journals such as *Early Child Development and Care, English Education, Equity and Excellence in Education, Journal of Early Childhood Literacy, Journal of Research in Childhood Education, Language Arts, Research in the Teaching of English, Teachers College Record*, and *Young Children*. She is a recipient of the American Educational Research Association (AERA) Language and Social Processes Early Career Award (2008), the AERA Early Education and Child Development Early Research Career Award (2009), the National Council for Research on Language and Literacy (NCRLL) Early Researcher Career Award (2009), the Kappa Delta Pi/AERA Division K (Teaching and Teacher Education) Early Career Award (2010), and the AERA Division K Innovations in Research on Diversity in Teacher Education Award (2011). She is the chair of AERA's Critical Perspectives in Early Childhood Education SIG (2013–2014), chair of NCTE's Early Childhood Education Assembly (2012–2014), and a trustee of the NCTE Research Foundation (2012–2015).